Ruth

God's Amazing Love for You

AN IN-DEPTH BIBLE STUDY

by Courtney Joseph
with Beverly Wise

Table of Contents

Preface

The story of Ruth and Boaz is one of the most beautiful examples of God's love and sovereignty recorded in the Bible.

As the book of Ruth begins, you will see two women who were facing the worst days of their lives. They could not have known how God was setting the stage for their greatest blessings to come.

If you have suffered the loss of a loved one or the loss of a dream, then you will know exactly how Ruth felt. Ruth's past could have held her back, but she courageously went forward with her life and let God direct her paths.

In this study, you will see that you do *not* have to have a perfect family to be used by God. You will see a friendship that is life changing, and you will see that nothing in life happens by accident.

Woven throughout this beautiful love story is a greater story of God's amazing love for us. In Week Five, we will take an in-depth look at how Boaz's love for Ruth is a picture of God's love for us. Be sure you finish Week Five, because like the finale of a fireworks show, it is simply the best!

I hope that this verse-by-verse study of the book of Ruth fills you to the brim with hope! Be sure to set aside at least 20 minutes a day for your study, and if you fall behind, use the weekends to catch up.

Let's begin this journey together as we walk with the King.

Courtney

Week 1~Introduction and Overview

Verse of the Day:

If any of you lacks wisdom,

Let him ask God, Who gives

generously to all.

James 1:5

Day One: Loss, Loyalty, Love, and Lineage

Who doesn't enjoy a good love story? The romance genre of books and movies is a billion-dollar industry, so I know I'm not alone.

Every winter, my daughter and I pop popcorn, cuddle up on the couch, and watch Hallmark Christmas movies. What is the common theme through all of these family-friendly movies? Romance. They are predictable, and that one little kiss at the end is always the best part!

As we begin our study through the book of Ruth, it's fun to note that this is a beautiful love story. Not only will there be a wedding at the end (so we can assume that includes a kiss), but there will also be a baby boy born.

However, this story is about much more than just love and lineage; this story begins with a terrible loss. Following Ruth's loss, she had a decision to make—and there is where we will see Ruth's loyalty. Not only is Ruth a good friend, but she is also a faithful follower of God.

Ruth's story is one of loss, loyalty, love, family lineage…and hope!

If you love God and want His will for your life, you will relate to Ruth.

If you have suffered the loss of a loved one or a dream, you will relate to Ruth.

If you have ever felt like your past might hold you back, you will relate to Ruth.

If you believe redemption is possible for your life no matter what you've gone through, you will relate to Ruth.

Let's get started on our 5-week journey—verse by verse, chapter by chapter—through the book of Ruth!

Your assignment for today is to read through all four chapters of the book of Ruth in one sitting. So grab your favorite drink, go to your favorite spot, curl up with a blanket, and enjoy! I'll see you back here in 15 minutes.

Now that you've completed your reading, take a moment to reflect on the entire story.

DISCUSSION QUESTIONS:

Who are the main characters in the book of Ruth?

What is your first overall impression from reading through the book of Ruth?

What insights has the Holy Spirit already revealed to you?

I'm so glad you have committed to studying the book of Ruth with us. Write a prayer of commitment to God below, asking Him to help you complete every page of this study.

We need the help of the Holy Spirit to speak God's truth into our hearts and minds as we read God's Word. James 1:5 says, *"If any of you lacks wisdom, let him ask God, who gives generously to all without reproach, and it will be given him."*

May God give us wisdom on this journey, and may we live well because we are drinking from the living well, the living words of God. Keep walking with the King.

Verse of the Day:

For where you go I will go,

and where you lodge I will lodge.

Your people shall be my people,

and your God my God.

Ruth 1:16

Day Two: A Committed Friend

There are only two books in the Bible named after women: Ruth and Esther. Both of these women had internal beauty. We do not know who the author of the book of Ruth is, but the genealogy in chapter four suggests it was written during or after the time of David. Jewish tradition credits Samuel as the author.

In the Hebrew Bible, the book of Ruth is grouped with Song of Solomon, Esther, Ecclesiastes, and Lamentations. Each of these books is associated with Israel's principal feasts and were read by rabbis on special occasions during the year. Ruth was read annually at the Feast of Weeks, also known as the Feast of Pentecost.

Two of the most beautiful verses in the entire Bible are found in Ruth chapter 1.

Write out Ruth 1:16–17 below.

These verses are often read at weddings, but in context, Ruth said this to her mother-in-law, Naomi.

The Hebrew word for Ruth means "friend" and "companion."

How do these verses relate to the meaning of Ruth's name?

What was the only thing that would part Ruth from Naomi?

Ruth was a woman of character who loved without barriers. Not only did she have an interracial marriage, she had an interracial friendship with Naomi. She was a committed friend because Naomi's God had become her God. Naomi's life would forever be changed because of this young woman's courage to commit her life to her.

Ruth and Naomi's friendship is a role model for our friendships with other women.

Ruth said: *"For where you go I will go, and where you lodge I will lodge."*

Perhaps you have a close friend who has moved away. Most likely you keep in touch through yearly visits, phone calls, and Christmas cards. Can you imagine making the commitment to move where she lives so she would never be alone? This was a huge sacrifice!

Ruth said: *"Your people shall be my people."*

Ruth and Naomi were different ages, races, and religions. How would this world be different if women broke down barriers and loved other women different than themselves?

Naomi's love for God gave Ruth a desire to know God. Ruth said, *"and your God my God."*

When people look at your life, do you think they say, "I want her God to be my God?" Do your friendships bring others closer to God?

Sometimes God uses sermons and good books and programs to change women's lives. But *the most effective tool for discipleship is friendship.* Friendships change lives. We can be tempted to run around doing a thousand different service projects and miss this truth. Your time, consistency, and presence in the life of a friend make a huge difference. It is within friendship where we can talk and walk and wrestle out our faith. It is powerful!

Over our lifetime, we will have a limited amount of time to invest in our friendships. So let's reflect on our friendships and make them matter.

DISCUSSION QUESTIONS:

List your closest friends.

How can you be more selfless as a committed friend?

What changes can you make to open yourself up to friendships that cross barriers like race, age, and religion?

How can you bring your friends closer to God simply through being a committed friend?

Ruth 4:15 says that Ruth's love was worth more than seven sons. In Hebrew culture, sons were highly valued, and the number seven symbolized perfection. So Ruth's friendship was better than Naomi having a perfect family!

If God is not central in our lives, we will be tempted to pursue a perfect family and a perfect life. The reality is, there are no perfect families or lives. The gospel frees us from this bondage of perfection and moves us into grace-filled relationships.

Let's choose love and living a committed life today. Close in prayer, and ask God to show you how you can be a better friend and draw others closer to God.

Verse of the Day:

But our citizenship is in heaven,

and from it we await a Savior,

the Lord Jesus.

Philippians 3:20

Day Three: A Heritage

When my kids were little, we took them to Ellis Island to see where my great-grandparents first arrived in America. We drove ten hours to Pennsylvania, and from there we took a train to Penn Station, a taxi to Battery Park, and a ferry to see the Statue of Liberty. From the Statue of Liberty, we boarded another ferry and finally made it to Ellis Island.

Did I mention we waited in line for nearly two hours to catch the ferry? Did I mention there was a security check that made us feel like criminals? Did I mention how we were all squished on the ferry to the island? As an impatient American, that was not my favorite experience of the day.

But God had a life lesson in store for me that day!

In the early 1900s, my great-grandfather came over on a boat from Hungary, so we stood where he once stood. As I read the history of the horrific month-long boat ride from Europe to the land of opportunity, I was humbled. The pictures of the travelers squished onto the boat, with only the clothes on their back and nothing but hope packed in their hearts, touched me.

Suddenly, the long car ride, train ride, taxi ride, line, security check, and ferry ride seemed minor compared to what my great-grandfather went through to see Lady Liberty!

My great-grandpa came with a dream—to make life better for generations to come; and there I stood, living out his dream. Could he have imagined how amazing his great-granddaughter's life would be—all because of his sacrifice?

Thank you, Lord, for such a brave and visionary great-grandfather!

RUTH'S HERITAGE:

While my grandpa came to America in hopes of a better life, today we will see that Ruth made a choice that did not necessarily mean she'd have a better life.

Read Ruth 1:4. Ruth was not Jewish. What was her nationality?

Read Genesis 19:30–38. What is the origin of the country of Moab?

This story is a troubling read. After God destroyed the city of Sodom and Gomorrah, the incestuous relations of Lot and his two daughters produced two sons, Moab and Ben-ammi. These sons formed the nations of the Moabites and the Ammonites.

Read Judges 3:12–14. What was the relationship like between Israel and the Moabites?

The Moabites and Ammonites were Israel's enemies. The Moabites oppressed Israel for 18 years during the time of the Judges.

Read 1 Kings 11:33. Who did the Moabites worship as their God?

Naomi and her sons immigrated to Moab to avoid death from the famine, and the very thing they feared happened. All three men died.

Since Ruth was a Moabite and the Moabites were bitter enemies of the Jews, you can see that Ruth was putting her life in danger by returning with her mother-in-law to Bethlehem.

Naomi was too old to work, too old to remarry, her only children were dead, and she had no land. She was in complete poverty. So Ruth was giving up her own life, her own name, and her own people to become a stranger in a foreign land. When Ruth chose to leave her country, she knew it might be a worse life.

We all know the end of the story; it all works out beautifully. But Ruth did not know the end of her story, yet she still chose the selfless way.

DISCUSSION QUESTIONS:

Put yourself in Ruth's shoes. After studying the history of her people, what sort of fears do you think Ruth had?

When you make decisions, do you tend to take the *selfless* route or the *selfish* route?

It is natural to think that the selfish route will make us happier, but when we choose to trust God and live selflessly, we are free and blessed.

What is your heritage? Did anyone have to make a sacrifice so you could live where you live today?

What is your spiritual heritage? Who made a sacrifice so you could be a child of God?

While I value my American citizenship and the sacrifice of my great-grandparents, I value even more my citizenship in heaven and the sacrifice of Jesus for my salvation.

Philippians 3:20–21 says, *"But our citizenship is in heaven, and from it we await a Savior, the Lord Jesus Christ, who will transform our lowly body to be like his glorious body, by the power that enables him even to subject all things to himself."*

Our citizenship is in heaven. This means that we are foreigners in this world, and our lives should look different than those who are *not* citizens of heaven. It means that we should love selflessly, even if it makes us uncomfortable. We have a great hope of heaven.

Let's close our study today by glancing at Matthew chapter 1. This is the genealogy of Jesus. Look specifically at verse 5. There are two women's names. Who are they?

Friends, this is grace at its best! Rahab, a prostitute, and Ruth, a Moabite, are both in the genealogy of Jesus Christ! Do you know what this means? This means it doesn't matter where you've come from or what you've done—God wants to use you. All He asks is for your complete surrender and a willingness to live selflessly for His glory.

Our citizenship is in heaven. Let's live for eternity!

Verse of the Day:

For the grace of God has appeared,

bringing salvation for all people.

Titus 2:11

Day Four: Dark Days

Today is our final day of overview. Tomorrow we will begin our verse-by-verse study through the book of Ruth.

Ruth lived during one of Israel's lowest points spiritually.

According to Ruth 1:1, when did the story of Ruth take place?

The book of Ruth occurred *during* the days of the judges, before Israel had kings to rule over them. Even though Ruth is placed in the Bible chronologically after the book of Judges, the events in Ruth occurred *during* these days.

The approximate dates when the judges ruled are 1400–1050 BC. The events in Ruth are believed to have occurred closer to the beginning of the 350-year period than the end of the period.

How does Judges 21:25 describe the culture in Israel during the days when the judges ruled?

If you read through the book of Judges, you will see that the nation of Israel was weak in its faith. They were disobedient to God and held to no absolutes.

"Everyone did what was right in his own eyes."

These were very dark days.

It is into this cultural setting that we see the lives of Ruth and Boaz lived out as examples of obedience, purity, and faith. Even in the darkest of times, God is always at work in the hearts and lives of those who are faithful to Him.

DISCUSSION QUESTIONS:

Read 2 Timothy 3:1–5. Do you think the times we are living in resemble the dark days of the judges from the past? Explain your answer.

How then should we as Christians commit to live our lives regardless of cultural norms?

Our times parallel the times of the judges, since today everyone is doing what is right in his own eyes. We must be careful to live obediently according to the Word of God so that we can continue to receive blessings and enjoy our relationship with God.

We need to be "lights" in an increasingly "dark" world.

As we study the book of Ruth, we will learn that even in the midst of our spiritually dark, sinful culture, as followers of Jesus Christ, we are to live out our faith to the glory of God. Our ultimate hope is in our Savior, our Redeemer, the Lord Jesus Christ.

Titus 2:11–14 says, *"For the grace of God has appeared, bringing salvation for all people, training us to renounce ungodliness and worldly passions, and to live self-controlled, upright, and godly lives in the present age, waiting for our blessed hope, the appearing of the glory of our great God and Savior Jesus Christ, who gave himself for us to redeem us from all lawlessness and to purify for himself a people for his own possession who are zealous for good works."*

Have you chosen to follow Jesus?

If you have not received Jesus Christ as your personal Savior, confess your sins (1 John 1:9), believe, and receive Him now. Jesus Christ is our only Hope!

Let's Pray.

Dear Heavenly Father,

You are so good. Thank you for the sacrifice of your Son and the forgiveness of our sins. Forgive us for putting our hope and trust in the wrong things. Please open our eyes and hearts to understand your word clearly. Help us to obey and honor you with our lives. Change us, and make us more like you.

In Jesus' name we pray, Amen.

Verse of the Day:

God is our refuge and strength,

an ever-present help in trouble.

Psalm 46:1

Day Five: Let's Begin

I remember back in my high school English class reading novels at home then discussing them later in class. I was always amazed at how much I would learn during our class discussions. I had missed much of the symbolism and underlying meanings when reading the book on my own. Sometimes I wondered if the book we were discussing in class was the same book I had read at home. I was such a literal reader that the figurative language fell flat on me, and I needed the insight of others to draw it out.

If you are new to the book of Ruth, you may miss some of the symbolism. That's okay! As we approach the end of the study, I will explain how Boaz is a picture of Jesus, acting in grace to redeem Ruth. There are also quite a few other interesting lessons woven into this book that we will see in the end.

The words *redeem*, *redeemer* and *kinsman-redeemer* are keywords in this book. They are used 20 times. Another keyword is LORD, which in Hebrew is Yahweh, and it is used 17 times. This is the covenant name for God.

Throughout this study, we are going to do some color-coding. The color-coding is completely optional; if you want to do this in your Bible, you may. If coloring in your Bible makes you uncomfortable, you can purchase a special Bible just for coloring in, print out the book of Ruth from the Internet, or skip this part of the study entirely. Do whatever works for you. The point of color-coding is to help us slow down and soak in God's Word as we read it carefully.

We will be using the English Standard Version (ESV) since it is a close word-for-word translation of the original scriptures. But you may use whatever version you prefer.

GMG BIBLE COLORING CHART

COLORS	KEYWORDS
PURPLE	God, Jesus, Holy Spirit, Saviour, Messiah
PINK	women of the Bible, family, marriage, parenting, friendship, relationships
RED	love, kindness, mercy, compassion, peace, grace
GREEN	faith, obedience, growth, fruit, salvation, fellowship, repentance
YELLOW	worship, prayer, praise, doctrine, angels, miracles, power of God, blessings
BLUE	wisdom, teaching, instruction, commands
ORANGE	prophecy, history, times, places, kings, genealogies, people, numbers, covenants, vows, visions, oaths, future
BROWN/GRAY	Satan, sin, death, hell, evil, idols, false teachers, hypocrisy, temptation

Let's begin!

In Ruth chapter 1, we will learn about two women, two countries, and two decisions. Go to God in prayer, asking God's Spirit to reveal His truth to you as you study His Word.

Now open your Bible to Ruth chapter 1. Slowly read verses 1 and 2 and color-code the verses. Mark them orange because these two verses cover history, time, place, and people.

We have already established that the events taking place in the book of Ruth occurred *"in the days when the judges ruled."* (Ruth 1:1) The nation of Israel was in steep spiritual decline because *"everyone did what was right in his own eyes."* (Judges 21:25)

As our story unfolds in chapter 1, we are given a window through which we see the lives of a family of four living in Judah during these dark days when the judges were ruling over the people of Israel.

According to Ruth 1:1, what happened in Judah to cause a man and his family to choose to leave their homeland and travel to a foreign country, remaining there for a period of time?

The famine must have been very severe for this family to leave their home to go and live in Moab.

Sometimes in the Old Testament, we see God withholding rain because the people in the land of Israel were being disobedient to God's Law. This drought would result in famine, and God used these times as discipline or judgment upon His people to bring them back to Him in repentance. An example of this can be seen in 1 Kings 17–18, during the days of Elijah.

Famines could also occur for other reasons. Please read Judges 6:1–6. What caused the famine for Israel according to these verses?

Once again, in the early days of the judges, the people of Israel did evil in the sight of the Lord, and there was military oppression and war. The Midianites would invade, stripping the land of all its produce and crops, which left the Israelites with very little food to eat.

The godly people as well as the ungodly people all suffered

According to verse 1, in what specific city in Judah is this family from?

Bethlehem was surrounded by grain fields that gave it its name, which means "House of Bread." But there was no bread in Bethlehem at this time because of the famine.

Bethlehem was located in the territory given to the tribe of Judah, about six miles south of Jerusalem. We are familiar with this city because it is the birthplace of the Lord Jesus Christ.

This family of four left Bethlehem and traveled to Moab, about 50 miles east on the other side of the Dead Sea. Obviously, there was no famine in Moab, and they probably only planned to live in Moab temporarily until the famine in Judah ended. We have seen that the nation of Moab had oppressed Israel, and they were a nation of idol worshipers.

How does God describe Moab in Psalm 60:8? (Repeated also in Psalm 108:9)?

The Amplified Bible says, "Moab is my wash pot." In other words, they are his footbath, fit for the lowest form of servitude.

God is reminding and reassuring His people Israel that He is in possession of the land, and He is sovereign, in charge of the nations.

What were the names of the four family members moving to Moab according to verse 2?

Hebrew names usually carried a meaning.

Elimelech, the father's name, means "my God is King," testifying to his faith in God.

Naomi, the mother's name, means "the pleasant one."

The son's names, Mahlon and Chilion, mean "the sick, weakling" and "the pining one." The sons' names could indicate they were unhealthy, sickly and weak.

Verse 2 tells us they were Ephrathites, which means "fruitful place." This is what the people were called who were from the region around Bethlehem-Ephrathah.

DISCUSSION QUESTIONS:

Naomi followed her husband's lead away from the Promised Land, into a foreign country with foreign customs. How do you think she felt in this new land?

Naomi's husband's choices led to her instability. Have you ever had a time when someone else's choices caused you to suffer? How did God show up in the midst of your suffering?

Our God's love is constant and never changing. Even on our hardest days, He is there with us and taking care of us. Sometimes we cannot see what is ahead or how He will provide for our needs or solve our problems. But He is there. Though this book of the Bible may be named after Ruth, this story is also about Naomi and how God lovingly took care of her. God cares for the least of these.

Continue to put your trust in God. He loves you!

"God is our refuge and strength, an ever-present help in trouble." —Psalm 46:1

Let's close out our week of Bible study in prayer.

Dear Heavenly Father,

Thank you for your Word and for what you have taught us this week. Help us to apply all that we have learned. Thank you for your loving care and constant presence in our lives. Help us to follow your lead and trust you more.

In the strong name of Jesus we pray, Amen.

Week 2~Ruth 1

Verse of the Day:

For we walk by faith,

Not by sight.

2 Corinthians 5:7

Day One: Walk by Faith
Ruth 1:1-5

Let's begin with prayer.

Slowly read or color-code Ruth 1:1–5.

There is no right or wrong way to do the coloring. It is simply a tool to help us slow down and soak in every Word of God. (Most of mine is orange and pink.)

Have you ever stood in line at the grocery store, sizing up the other lines? You get into one line, and it seems to be moving very slowly, so you change to a line that appears to be going faster. Then you discover that you would have been better off if you had stayed in the original line.

The same thing always happens to me on the highway. If there is a slowdown, I will inevitably switch lanes to try to find a faster lane—and end up in a slower lane.

In our reading today, we saw Elimelech moving his family to Moab in hopes of a better life. Instead, their life there was very difficult. Even though they would have had enough food to eat, as immigrants, they had no legal rights, could not purchase or own land, and would have been forced to work for very low wages. Economically speaking, they would have been at the bottom of the scale and very poor.

DISCUSSION QUESTIONS:

Elimelech faced a difficult decision regarding the welfare of his family. Do you think he made the right decision moving his family into a pagan land so that they would have food to eat? Or do you think he should have stayed in Bethlehem, waited for the famine to end, and trusted God to provide for the needs of his family?

Was Elimelech doing "what was right in his own eyes" rather than trusting God? Do you think his faith was weak?

Read 2 Corinthians 5:7. What does this verse teach us about how God wants us to live?

God wants us to put our faith and trust in Him.

Elimelech looked only at what his eyes could see—his present difficult circumstances. Scripture doesn't tell us that he prayed or sought the Lord's direction before moving his family to Moab. He saw a lack of food and chose to provide for his family's needs in his own way. Perhaps there were other options.

He could have stayed with the others who remained in Bethlehem, patiently waiting for the famine to end. Or they could have crossed the Jordan River, going east into the region where other Jewish tribes had settled (the Reubenites, Gadites, and tribe of Manasseh) rather than going into the pagan nation of Moab.

How do you tend to "walk" through your life? Do you walk by faith or by sight? What are some examples of times when you walked by faith or walked by sight, and what happened?

Look at verse 4. How many years did they stay in Moab?

Do you think the family stayed much longer than they intended?

Look at verses 3–5. What personal tragedies struck Naomi's family?

Scripture doesn't record how any of these men died.

Look at verse 4. Both of Elimelech's sons, Mahlon and Chilion, were married before their deaths. Whom did they marry?

Look ahead at Ruth 4:10. Which son was Ruth married to?

Read Deuteronomy 7:1–4. Mahlon and Chilion were Jewish men. Was it okay for Jewish men to intermarry?

Read 2 Corinthians 6:14–18. Does the New Testament also teach that Christians should separate themselves from unbelievers? Could this principle be applied to our marriages, business associations, or partnerships?

Christians are not to be bound together with unbelievers, but the Apostle Paul was not saying that Christians should not have any contact or relationships with unbelievers. Otherwise, how could we share the Gospel with them and lead them to Jesus Christ as their Savior? Our marriages, our business partnerships, and our spiritual relationships, however, are meant to give glory to God, and Scripture clearly teaches that "we are not to be unequally yoked."

Returning to Ruth, we have seen three deaths and three grieving widows. These were heartbreaking and difficult circumstances for each of these women. Even more tragic was the fact that there were no sons or grandsons to carry on the family name and legal rights.

Most of us have experienced the death of a loved one, so we can imagine what it would have been like for Naomi to lose not only her husband, but also both of her sons while living in a foreign land. What grief she must have felt while burying three family members. Her sorrow must have been overwhelming.

But God!

God is faithful, and He was faithful with Naomi. We are about to see a beautiful plan unfold for her life and the life of Ruth.

"Wait for the LORD; be strong, and let your heart take courage; wait for the LORD!" — Psalm 27:14

If you are walking through a valley right now, wait on the Lord. Walk by faith. God is with you. Hold onto hope, and keep walking with the King.

Verse of the Day:

One generation shall commend your works to another.

Psalm 145:4

Day Two: Loving Your Familiy
Ruth 1:6-9

Let's begin with prayer.

Slowly read or color-code Ruth 1:6–9.

Remember, there is no right or wrong way to do the coloring. It is simply a tool to help us slow down and soak in every Word of God.

We have all heard the stories about—or perhaps even experienced—a controlling, meddling, or manipulative mother-in-law. Sadly, it is more common to hear about tense and difficult in-laws than it is to hear about good ones. For some, at the start of marriage, things were fine. But once the children came along, expectations increased—and so did the conflicts.

This is not God's will. God meant for parents to be a loving support system for their grown children and grandchildren. We are to recount God's faithfulness and love from one generation to the next.

"One generation shall commend your works to another, and shall declare your mighty acts." —Psalm 145:4

The Bible gives us several examples of supportive in-laws.

Read Luke 4:38–40. What did Simon Peter's mother-in-law do immediately after she was healed?

Read Exodus 18:17–24. What did Moses' father-in-law give him in verse 19?

Naomi is another good example. Naomi and her daughters-in-law had a deep affection for one another, and clearly the bond of widowhood had drawn them even closer to one another.

According to verse 6, why did Naomi decide to return from Moab to her homeland of Judah after the death of her husband and sons?

In verse 6, we see that Naomi had heard the good news that the Lord had visited His people and given them food. The famine in Judah had ended. The fact that the Lord had "visited His people," probably by sending rain so that the crops and fruit would grow, shows the sovereignty of God over nations and His control over nature.

God showed mercy to His people and gave them food once again.

As Naomi set out on her journey back to Bethlehem, both of her daughters-in-law accompanied her.

According to verse 8, what did Naomi advise her daughters-in-law to do?

Look at verses 8, 11, 12 and 15. How many times did Naomi encourage them to turn back to their own homes?

Why do you think she may have given that advice?

Most likely Naomi was being thoughtful of them, urging them to remarry and find rest in the house of their future husbands. Also, the prospect of finding husbands in Judah would have been slim since Ruth and Orpah were Moabite women, so Naomi thought it best for them to stay in Moab where opportunities for remarriage would have been greater.

In verses 8 and 9, Naomi prays a prayer of blessing over Orpah and Ruth. In verse 8, she says, *"May the LORD (referring to Jehovah, the God of Israel) deal kindly with you, as you have dealt with the dead and with me."*

The word "kindness" in Hebrew is the word, "hesed." This is an important word in the Old Testament. It is speaking about God's faithful covenant love and loyalty to His people, Israel. Because Ruth and Orpah had married Jewish men and been gracious to them and their mother-in-law, she wanted God to be "kind" to them in return.

In ancient times, widows lacked security, and most were economically needy.

Naomi knew if God granted each of them another husband, Ruth and Orpah would have security and rest, a family, and a home, which was especially important for women in the culture in which they lived.

Naomi showed love and concern for her daughters-in-law as she affectionately kissed them goodbye, and they all wept together. The two young widows could not comprehend leaving Naomi because they so deeply loved her.

DISCUSSION QUESTIONS:

Have you ever wept when you said goodbye to a loved one? Who was that person, and what were you feeling as you said goodbye?

Now imagine these three women saying their goodbyes. What does their relationship teach us about mothers-in-law and daughters-in-law?

Naomi selflessly wanted what was best for her daughters-in-law, even though she may have wanted to take them back to Bethlehem to keep them close to her. She was willing to sacrifice her own needs for theirs so they could have what Naomi thought would be a brighter future. In return, Orpah and Ruth were willing to sacrifice their own future security of a husband, home, and family in Moab because of their good and loving relationship with their mother-in-law.

May we be inspired today to follow Ruth and Naomi's example, and may we be loving, loyal, and committed to building the best relationship possible with our extended families.

Verse of the Day:

And we know that for those

who love God all things

work together for good.

Romans 8:28

Day Three: Finding Rest
Ruth 1:10-13

Let's begin with prayer.

Slowly read or color-code Ruth 1:10–13.

As we begin today's reading, I want to look back at verse 9 for a moment. In this verse, Naomi told her daughters-in-law that she wanted the Lord to grant them rest with a new husband. While God had not provided husbands for security and rest, God was with them. God was their shelter, their provider, their security, and their rest. There is no one greater than our God!

In verses 10–12, when Orpah and Ruth objected to returning to their homes, what reason did Naomi use to try to discourage them from going back to Bethlehem with her?

In verse 12, Naomi cited her age, saying, "I am too old to have a husband." Most commentators think Naomi was about 50 years old which was past the age of childbearing. Naomi had little chance of having more sons, so she could not provide new husbands for Orpah and Ruth, even if they were willing to patiently wait for newborn sons to grow into manhood.

Possibly, Naomi was thinking of the custom in Israel of a levirate marriage in which it was a brother's responsibility to marry his deceased brother's childless widow. This was in order to conceive a son to carry on his brother's family name.

Read Deuteronomy 25:5–6. What does this Old Testament custom tell us about the importance of the family to God?

God places a high priority and value on marriage and the family. God designed marriage to be between one man and one woman. God also said the man and the woman were to be "fruitful and multiply." (Genesis 1:27–28 and Genesis 2:24).

DISCUSSION QUESTIONS:

Looking again at Ruth 1:12–13, do you think Naomi had lost hope because of the difficult, bitter circumstances she'd endured during her last 10 years living in Moab?

Did she blame God for the painful loss of her husband and two sons? Explain your answer.

Naomi was not necessarily blaming God, but she was describing how the hand of the Lord had worked in her life. She seemed to understand the sovereignty of God and attributed the tragic loss of her husband and two sons to Him. Naomi felt that God had afflicted her, and she was in deep grief. Even though her circumstances were exceedingly bitter, she had not lost her faith and hope in God.

If Naomi had been bitter towards God, she would not have returned to the God of Israel. And since she knew that His hand could go out *against* her, she also knew it could be *for* her. What Naomi didn't know was how greatly God's hand was for her!

Have you personally seen God's hand at work in your own life? In what ways?

How does seeing Naomi's faith help you to hold onto hope, even in the midst of difficult circumstances?

We must cling to the promises of the Word of God as we go through trying times.

Romans 8:28 states, *"And we know that for those who love God all things work together for good, for those who are called according to his purpose."*

God is sovereign over every event that occurs in our lives, whether joyful or sorrowful. God has a plan and a purpose for each of our lives, and He will accomplish it for our good and His glory. We can be confident of that!

In the book of Genesis, we see God created the family. Family is God's idea! In verse 9, Naomi called a new marriage for her daughters-in-law a place of "rest." Marriage—and family—is meant to be a place of rest. It is meant to be a place where we love selflessly and care for one another's needs.

For those today who are hurting with broken marriages and families, God has also given us the church. God is our Heavenly Father, and we are His children. We are all brothers and sisters in Christ, and we are to selflessly love and care for one another within the family of God.

Take the time today to love on those in your physical and spiritual family. Enjoy the rest that comes from these God-given relationships.

Verse of the Day:

For where you go I will go,

and where you lodge I will lodge.

Your people shall be my people,

and your God my God.

Ruth 1:16

Day Four: Counting the Cost
Ruth 1:14-18

Let's begin with prayer.

Slowly read or color-code Ruth 1:14–18.

Which daughter-in-law accepted Naomi's advice, and which one wisely rejected it?

Back in verse 10, both women said they would go with Naomi, but now that it's truly time to go, we see Orpah change her mind. Once she considered the high cost of staying with Naomi, she decided to return to her people and her gods and their ways. We see this sometimes in church when people make a commitment to Christ. Sometimes during an emotional moment, someone will say a prayer or walk an aisle or raise their hand to be saved. But once they return home to their people and their old familiar ways, their emotional decision becomes too high of a cost—they weren't truly committed.

As the women wept together, Orpah kissed Naomi goodbye, knowing that they would never see each other again.

Orpah made the wrong decision to stay with the people of Moab and would continue worshiping her godless, pagan idols. Ruth, on the other hand, "clung" to Naomi. In Hebrew, this word has the same meaning as the word "cleave," which means to stick like glue.

Ruth chose to glue herself to Naomi, to follow her and put her faith in the true God of Israel, turning away from the godless idols of Moab.

Read verses 16–18. Did Ruth make an emotional decision, or did she consider the cost of her commitment?

Ruth refused to take Naomi's advice to remain in Moab. Remember, Ruth had lost her husband too, along with her father-in-law and brother-in-law. We do not know when it happened, but somewhere over the course of the 10 years, God had used Naomi and her family to draw Ruth to Himself. Ruth had come to faith in the God of Israel, Yahweh, the true and living God.

This is interesting for two reasons:

Reason # 1: Everyone who is not a Jew is a Gentile. Ruth was a Gentile, so this shows us that God's plan of redemption is not only for the Jews, but also for the Gentiles.

Reason # 2: Ruth was a Moabite. No Moabite, even to the tenth generation, was to enter the assembly of God. This was because the Moabites did not meet Israel with food and water when they came out of Egyptian bondage. The Moabites also hired Balaam to try to curse Israel, but God did not allow Balaam to be successful (Deuteronomy 23:3–5).

So how could Ruth, a Moabite woman, be saved by God if she could not enter the assembly of God? One possible explanation is that Ruth was born after the eleventh generation.

What do you learn about God's heart in I Timothy 2:3–4?

What do you learn about God's heart in 2 Peter 3:9?

These verses show us God's grace and mercy toward all people, Jews and Gentiles alike. His heart's desire is that all will turn to Him in repentance of sin and put their faith in His Son, Jesus Christ.

DISCUSSION QUESTIONS:

When you placed your faith in Christ, was it an emotional decision or a lifelong commitment?

What has your faith cost you?

Is there any part of your heart that sometimes longs for the world or your old ways?

Commit today to follow God wherever He leads you, no matter the cost.

Let's look at Ruth's commitment in verses 16 and 17. What specific promises did Ruth make to Naomi? List them.

What character traits of Ruth do you admire and desire to imitate in either your own relationship with God or with others?

Ruth is an admirable woman, and the same traits we see in Ruth we see first in Christ.

Jesus' love is selfless and sacrificial. Jesus emptied Himself, and He took the form of a servant, humbled Himself, and became obedient to the point of death, even death on a cross (Philippians 2:5–8).

Jesus showed kindness and was often moved with compassion for people (Mark 6:34).

Jesus was determined. He began to show His disciples that He must go to Jerusalem and suffer many things from the elders and chief priests and scribes, be killed, and on the third day be raised (Matthew 16:21).

Jesus is loyal and committed to those who are His. He promises that He will never, ever leave us or forsake us. Also, we are eternally secure in Him when we have put our faith in Him as our personal Lord and Savior (Hebrews 13:5).

We need to examine ourselves to see if we, like Jesus and Ruth, are practicing and demonstrating all of these characteristics in our own lives with the people we love and the God we serve.

In closing, Ruth asked God to hold her accountable to keep her vow. Sensing Ruth's determination and the seriousness of her vow, Naomi became silent and said no more to her. May we be like Ruth, committed to following Christ no matter the cost

Verse of the Day:

May the God of hope fill you with

all joy and peace in believing,

so that by the power of the Holy Spirit

you may abound in hope.

Romans 15:13

Day Five: Finding Hope
Ruth 1:19-22

Let's begin with prayer.

Read or color-code Ruth 1:19–22.

We all have had bad things happen in our lives that we had no control over. While we may not be able to control how others treat us or the hard things that God allows in our lives, we can control our *response.* If we respond to our hurt and wounding with anger, over time that anger will turn into bitterness. Bitterness is not only a sin, but it will take a toll on us both emotionally and physically. I hope that by the end of today's lesson you will find hope in the midst of your hurts and be restored in your soul as well.

In these last verses of chapter 1, we see that Ruth's words matched her actions, giving evidence of her faith. Ruth set out from Moab with Naomi to begin a new life in Bethlehem. The journey would have taken the two women the better part of a week to travel since it was about 50 miles to Bethlehem.

As Naomi and Ruth entered Bethlehem, we are told that the whole town was stirred or abuzz about their return.

What question did the women of the town ask?

Why might they have asked that question?

The women seemed surprised by Naomi's appearance. Naomi had been gone for ten years, and those years had been hard and filled with tragedy. Most likely it showed in her appearance.

She and Elimelech may have been influential in the town before they left, and now Naomi returns in poverty, bringing with her a young foreign woman, a Moabite. That must have made the women very curious!

How did Naomi respond to the women?

In verse 20, Naomi asked her friends to no longer call her Naomi, which means "pleasant." Instead, she asked them to call her Mara, which means "bitter." Naomi's circumstances had gone from pleasant to bitter, and she felt that name better suited her now.

To whom did Naomi attribute her bitter, difficult circumstances? What does Naomi seem to understand?

In verses 20–21, Naomi referred to God as the "Almighty." In Hebrew, the word is *Shadday*, taken from the root word *shadad*, which means powerful.

Naomi was emphasizing God's power at work in her life and that the bitter circumstances and suffering she'd endured were from God being personally involved in her life. She recognized the sovereign hand of Almighty God.

How did Naomi view the last ten years of her life?

She went away from Bethlehem "full," with a husband and two sons, and had possibly taken many earthly possessions with her. But the Lord had brought her back from Moab "empty."

She'd lost much over the course of the ten years—her husband, two sons, and possibly all of her earthly goods which she may have had to sell because of the poverty widows faced in ancient times. However, one thing that Naomi failed to recognize about her situation was that she had not returned completely "empty" because she had her faithful daughter-in-law, Ruth, with her.

At what time of the year did Naomi return to Bethlehem?

Verse 22 tells us she arrived "at the beginning of barley harvest." This would have been the first of Israel's harvests in the springtime, which usually occurred in late April, early May. For the people of Judah, this would have been a time of rejoicing when praise was given to God for His provision of food.

Remember, Naomi left because there was a famine in the land, but she returned to a bountiful harvest. There was no more famine. Instead, there was now hope ahead for these two widows, Ruth and Naomi, because of the grace, mercy, and favor that God was about to bestow upon them.

This is the character of our God! He never leaves us without hope.

Our hope is in God and God alone.

DISCUSSION QUESTIONS:

Have you ever felt empty, hopeless, and bitter like Naomi?

Where do we need to go to find our hope?

What do you learn in Romans 15:13?

When storms hit and trials come into our lives, raw emotions bubble up under the surface and begin to overflow. We begin to ask God questions, and we wonder, "Does He care? Does God love me? Is He in control?"

Is God in control of everything? Yes, a thousand times yes!

When we put our faith in Jesus Christ as our Lord and Savior, He alone is the source of our hope. He will fill us with joy and peace, and we will overflow with hope through the power of the Holy Spirit.

Every page of scripture points to a sovereign God; from the Creation account in Genesis to the return of Christ in Revelation, our God is in complete control. And we are about to see our sovereign God unfold His beautiful plan for the lives of Ruth and Naomi as chapter 2 begins. Until next week, keep walking with the King, and remember God loves you!

Week 3~Ruth 2

Verse of the Day:

It is more blessed to give than to receive.

Acts 20:35

Day One: God Cares for the Poor
Ruth 2:1-2

Let's begin with prayer.

Slowly read or color-code Ruth 2:1–2.

We see in today's reading the character of our God. He cares for the poor. Most of us will never know what it feels like not to know where our next meal will come from even while there are people across the world without dinner today. As we look at today's reading, may we remember to reflect God's heart and give to the poor.

Chapter 1 of Ruth closed by telling us that Naomi and her daughter-in-law, the Moabite, had arrived in Bethlehem at the beginning of the barley harvest, which occurred during the spring harvesting. As chapter 2 opens, our third main character in the book of Ruth enters the scene.

Who was this person, and what do you learn about him in verse 1?

His name was Boaz, and his name means "in him is strength." Boaz was a relative of Naomi's deceased husband and was of the clan of Elimelech. This fact will be very important to our story later.

Boaz is described as a "worthy" (ESV) and "mighty" (KJV) man. The Hebrew word for "mighty" is *gibbor*, which means powerful and "a mighty man of valor." This implies that Boaz was influential, powerful, capable, prominent, and wealthy.

As we stated earlier, in ancient times, most widows lived in poverty. In order to survive, Naomi and Ruth would need food to eat.

Because Ruth loved Naomi and wanted to serve and care for her, what did she volunteer to do according to verse 2?

Ruth respectfully asked Naomi's permission to look for a field where she would find favor to glean among the ears of grain with other impoverished people. Naomi gave Ruth permission and said, "Go, my daughter," showing the affection and closeness of their relationship.

The word "glean" is repeated 11 times in chapter 2, so we need to understand this keyword. Gleanings were the stalks of grain left by the reapers after the first cutting. The needy—especially widows, orphans, and strangers—were allowed to pick up the grain that was left behind by the reapers.

Where did this plan for the leftover grain to be given to the poor and less fortunate originate? Look at Leviticus 19:9–10 and Deuteronomy 24:19–21.

God is the one who blessed Israel with bountiful harvests. It was God who instructed Israel through the Mosaic Law to provide for the needy. It is interesting to note that God did not give the needy a "handout"; they had to work hard in the hot sun doing the work of gleaning if they wanted food to eat.

DISCUSSION QUESTIONS:

No work should be considered too lowly. What warning did the Apostle Paul give in 2 Thessalonians 3:10b?

According to Colossians 3:23, how were the members of the church at Colossae encouraged to work by the Apostle Paul?

What do these verses tell us about the heart of God?

God cares about our needs. He showed concern for those who were less fortunate in Israel's society by commanding those who had an abundance to be generous and share with others so that none would go hungry.

As Christians, we should also meet the needs of those who are less fortunate. As those in the Old Testament were instructed by God to leave some grain behind for those who would glean, we too are to supply from our abundance to help others in their time of need. When given the opportunity, the less fortunate can also share in the work in order to help provide for their own needs and the needs of their families.

What are some practical examples of ways to care for others in need?

Here are some ideas to add to your list:

- In the summer, those who plant gardens could sow an extra row to donate their surplus food to their local food bank.

- At Christmas time, we could adopt a needy family and help to make Christmas special for them, as well as share the gospel with them.

- We could use our vehicle to transport those who need rides to work, doctor appointments, or church.

- We could provide backpacks filled with school supplies to children in need.

- We could take meals to the sick or the elderly or help provide food for a funeral dinner.

- We could set up a babysitting co-op for young families in our church to provide them a much-needed break.

- We could help someone with their yard work or household repairs.

As you can see, needs do not always have to be met monetarily. We can give of our time or use other resources to encourage and lift burdens.

Share a time when you helped meet someone's need, the manner in which you helped meet their need, and how God blessed you for your generosity.

Acts 20:35 tells us, "*In all things I have shown you that by working hard in this way we must help the weak and remember the words of the Lord Jesus, how he himself said, 'It is more blessed to give than to receive.'*"

When we are convinced that God will provide for our own needs, we find the freedom to give. We know God will take care of us as we take care of others. So if God is moving in your heart today to give, do it! As Acts 20:35 says, you will be blessed.

Verse of the Day:

The Lord be with you!

Ruth 2:4

Day Two: God Guides and Provides
Ruth 2:3-9

Let's begin with prayer.

Slowly read or color-code Ruth 2:3–9.

Most of the romantic movies that I watch are often predictable. When I watch these types of movies I always think, *None of that kind of stuff happens in real life.* But in today's reading, it does happen for Ruth and Boaz!

Nothing happens by accident for the children of God. God is always at work in our lives for our good and His glory. There is nothing this past week that happened in your life that was by chance, luck, or accidental. Let's look at an amazing story of God's sovereignty in the life of Ruth.

In verse 3, we are told that Ruth set out to find a field in which to glean. Remember, Ruth was a foreigner, so she would not have known what field to go to or who owned the various fields. It also appears—from looking ahead to 2:19—that Naomi did not direct Ruth to go to a particular field in which to work and glean.

Observing verse 3, whose part of the field did Ruth find to glean in? Who do you think directed her to that particular field, and why?

Verse 3 says that Ruth "happened" to come to the part of the field belonging to Boaz, who was of the clan of Elimelech. Ruth did not "happen" upon this field by accident or random chance. It is clear that God in His sovereignty guided Ruth to work and glean in the field owned by Boaz.

What does verse 3 teach us about the heart of God?

God was going to provide for Ruth and Naomi's needs through Boaz. As widows, they were in a vulnerable position, and God—without them realizing it yet—was guiding them and meeting their needs

DISCUSSION QUESTIONS:

Does God still work in our lives and guide us today? What do you learn in Philippians 2:13?

Can you give an example from your own life where God was clearly at work, guiding you to accomplish His plan and purpose for you?

From your observation of verse 4, how do you know that both Boaz and his workers (reapers) were godly men and enjoyed a good employer/employee relationship?

The way that Boaz and his workers greeted one another shows their godliness and their true care for one another. God is the first thing on their minds, and they know that He is the one who gives the harvest. Their faith in God is evident by their words to one another.

Now look at the timing. Boaz came from Bethlehem to visit his field at the same time that Ruth is there. This is how our God works! Consider the people you have met over the course of your lifetime. God has been orchestrating your life from birth.

In verse 5 we see that Boaz notices a young woman gleaning. Ruth must have stood out from the others, perhaps because she was a foreigner—or perhaps because she was beautiful.

According to verse 7, how had Ruth shown respect, and what kind of worker was she?

We see in this passage that Ruth is a Proverbs 31 woman. She has gotten up early and worked hard all day long with very few breaks. We will read later that she carries a very heavy load of barley home. Her arms were strong for the task. She has worked hard not just for herself, but to care for her mother-in-law as well.

This is convicting to me because I really don't like an entire day of hard manual labor. I like lots of breaks, snacks, and time to scroll through social media. Ruth is a great example of a godly woman who is willing to work hard, and God honored her hard work.

In verse 8, we see that Boaz took the initiative to meet and speak to Ruth.

In their culture, it would have been inappropriate for a woman, Ruth, to speak to Boaz first, especially because she was considered a lowly, impoverished Moabite widow, and Boaz was a great man in Bethlehem.

Look at verse 8. How did Boaz address Ruth? What did he call her? What might this tell us about their age difference?

Boaz called Ruth "my daughter" which implies there is a difference in their ages.

In verse 5, Boaz asked, "Whose young woman is this?" pointing out Ruth's youthfulness. It is believed that Boaz was an older man, probably closer to Naomi and Elimelech's age, since he saw Ruth as "a daughter" like Naomi did.

Many commentators believe Boaz was either a widower or never married. Ruth 3:10 also affirms that Boaz was most likely older because he praised Ruth for not going after younger men.

Look at verses 8 and 9. What did Boaz invite Ruth to do, and how did Boaz provide protection for her?

Boaz is a picture of Christ here. Boaz told Ruth to continue to glean in his field and not to leave his field for another one. He also instructed Ruth to keep close to the young women who worked in his field so she could get the best of the gleanings. Boaz further charged the young men not to touch Ruth, providing protection for her.

When she was thirsty, Boaz also gave Ruth the privilege of drinking water that had been drawn by the young men working for Boaz. This is shocking! In their culture, women filled the water jars for men, but here the men were serving Ruth.

Like Christ, Boaz sought out and served Ruth.

"For the Son of Man came to seek and to save the lost." —Luke 19:10

"For even the Son of Man came not to be served but to serve, and to give his life as a ransom for many." —Mark 10:45

Just as Boaz told Ruth to stay in his fields, God wants us to stay in His fields. We have no need to go wandering off into other fields, seeking fulfillment elsewhere. The world will dangle other fields in front of us such as success, pleasure, or money. But these fields are dangerous. God has provided protection and everything we need with Him. Do not wander off.

Be still.

Rest in His care of you.

Jesus loves you.

Verse of the Day:

May a full reward be given you

by the LORD, the God of Israel,

under whose wings you have

come to take refuge.

Ruth 2:12

Day Three: The Stage is Set
Ruth 2:10-13

Let's begin with prayer.

Slowly read or color-code Ruth 2:10–13.

It's an age-old question: *Why do bad things happen to good people?*

Have you ever wondered why bad things happen to you? Perhaps you struggle with fear, doubt, worry, anxiety, sleepless nights, or unanswered prayers!

All of these things can put a death grip on you and threaten to destroy your hope and joy. But let me assure you. I know that God is good, and we can trust in God's goodness even when what we are facing is not good.

The one question we never see Ruth asking is why all of this trouble and hardship has come her way. Instead, in today's passage, we will see her asking Boaz, "Why have I found favor in your eyes?"

Ruth has a beautiful attitude of trusting in God and a humility that recognizes that all good favor is a gift from God.

Looking at verse 10, what was Ruth's response to all of this generosity and kindness from Boaz?

Ruth showed total humility and gratitude as she bowed before Boaz with her face to the ground, which was a common gesture in the ancient Near East. Boaz was a very important, prominent man, and she was of a much lower social rank, a foreigner. Ruth showed respect and honor as she accepted his favor towards her.

The word "favor" is used three times in this chapter—in verses 2, 10, and 13. The Hebrew word is *chen*, which means graciousness and kindness. Boaz was moved to show favor, grace, and kindness to Ruth.

When someone has shown you favor, grace, generosity or kindness, how have you responded?

God has extended His graciousness and favor toward us through the gift of His Son, Jesus. Have you humbly bowed before Him and thanked him for His undeserved favor and grace?

Philippians 2:9–10 says, *"Therefore God has highly exalted him and bestowed on him the name that is above every name, so that at the name of Jesus every knee should bow, in heaven and on earth and under the earth."*

If you have not bowed your knee to the Lord and Savior, do it now.

Boaz gave favor and grace to Ruth during the days of the judges. Remember, we stated earlier that this was a time when the people of God had spiraled down into sin, yet Boaz chose to live a different lifestyle. He lived counter to his culture; he was a righteous man and obeyed the Mosaic Law.

God always has a righteous remnant living in sinful times.

DISCUSSION QUESTIONS:

How do you live counter to your culture? Do you daily seek to obey God's will according to His Word, whether it is "politically correct" or the popular thing to do? Can others see through your righteous living that you are a righteous woman?

We all need to pray that God will give us the courage to live out our Biblical convictions to God's glory, no matter the cost to us personally.

Ruth asked Boaz why all of this was happening to her; why had she found favor in his eyes? According to verse 11, how did Boaz respond to her question?

Bethlehem was a small town. If you remember from chapter 1:19, the whole town was stirred upon Naomi and Ruth's arrival from Moab. Obviously, Boaz had been told the details and the circumstances of their return and was made aware of Ruth's care for Naomi. Boaz admired and commended her for her devotion to her mother-in-law.

Look at verse 12. What did Boaz ask the Lord for?

What a beautiful prayer. Boaz did not just ask that she be rewarded but that she have a full reward—that her cup would be filled to the top, and that she'd be repaid in full for her full obedience to the Lord.

The best part of this prayer is that Boaz himself is about to become the answer!

In verse 12, what is the imagery used to describe Ruth's relationship with God?

For a baby bird, the wings of the mother provide safety and security. Ruth had chosen to trust God, to place herself under the care and protection of the Lord, and God was showing himself as faithful.

What was Ruth's response in verse 13?

And so the romance begins.

Boaz has encouraged her, and he has spoken words of kindness and comfort to her. Ruth has responded with gratefulness, and the stage is set!

When mealtime comes, Boaz will go beyond the Mosaic Law of caring for the poor, and he will invite Ruth to his dinner table. Their first date will begin!

Our God is an awesome God. His timing is perfect. If you are hurting today, trust God's timing and take refuge under his protective wings as you wait. God is with you, and He loves you.

Verse of the Day:

And she ate until she was satisfied.

Ruth 2:14

Day Four: Ruth and Boaz's First Date
Ruth 2:14-16

Let's begin with prayer.

Slowly read or color-code Ruth 2:14–16.

Have you ever been to one of those Italian Restaurants where they pour the oil in the bowl so you can dip your bread into it? Mmmm...so good!

At the end of yesterday's reading, the stage was set for Boaz and Ruth's first date. What was his pick-up line?

"Come here and eat some bread and dip your morsel in the wine." (v. 14)

Oh, I like this guy! I'm a girl who likes her carbs! I can just imagine how Ruth's heart must have skipped a beat with this invitation.

Boaz continued to go beyond the Mosaic Law by offering hospitality, generosity, and protection to Ruth.

According to verse 14, when mealtime came, where did Ruth sit?

Boaz invited Ruth to eat the meal with his reapers. It is interesting to note that Boaz ate and drank with his servants. He had more than a master/servant relationship with his workers. He was not embarrassed or ashamed to be seen eating a meal with his hired help.

How much did Ruth eat?

Ruth ate until she was satisfied. Let's pause here for a moment and take note. She was a woman of self-control. Though there was an abundance of food, she did not overeat.

When I'm at those restaurants with the bread and oil, I find myself tempted to eat more than I am truly hungry for. Ruth is a great example here of a woman who knew when she was physically full and stopped eating.

How do we know that Ruth was not a wasteful person? What did she do with her leftover food? (Look at 2:18)

Ruth did not throw her food away but took her leftovers home to give to Naomi to eat. Once again, verse 18 points out that she only ate until she was satisfied. This meant she had more to share with someone in need.

In Mark 6:34–44 we read about a time when Jesus miraculously fed a large crowd of people who had been listening to His teaching all day long. It was late in the day, and the people were hungry, but they had brought nothing to eat with them. With only five loaves and two fish, Jesus gave thanks to God for His provision of food and began breaking the loaves and dividing the fish. He then gave these to His disciples to distribute among the people.

The bread and fish were miraculously multiplied.

According to Mark 6:42–44, how many people were fed, how abundant was the provision of food, and what was done with the leftovers?

Five thousand men were fed. They all ate and were fully satisfied. Twelve baskets full of leftovers were gathered up after the meal. During the time of Jesus' ministry, a similar event was recorded in Mark 8:1–9. Here, also, the leftovers were gathered up after everyone had eaten and was satisfied.

DISCUSSION QUESTIONS:

What can we learn from the example of Jesus and Ruth in these passages of Scripture?

God has blessed us by providing food for our physical bodies. We are to eat only until we are satisfied. If we have an abundance of food, we are to be good stewards of our leftovers. We do not want to waste anything that God has given to us.

How did Boaz instruct his workers when Ruth returned to gleaning in the field after her meal? (See verses 15–16)

Sheaves were bundles of grain stalks tied together for transport to the threshing floor. Boaz told his workers to allow Ruth to glean among the sheaves. The workers were instructed to deliberately pull out from the stalks of barley extra grain and drop it in Ruth's path so that she would have an abundant amount provided for her. Also, the young men were not to "reproach" or "rebuke" her.

The word *reproach* means to taunt, insult, or to put to shame. And the word *rebuke* means to chide or reprove. So the young men working for Boaz were not to harass Ruth by taunting or insulting her or to hinder her in any way from gleaning in the field.

Many wonder why Boaz took a personal interest in Ruth by showing her such extraordinary care and kindness. One possible explanation is because of his own family tree.

Read Matthew 1:5. Who was the mother of Boaz?

Rahab is one of five women mentioned in the genealogy of Jesus Christ.

Look up Joshua 2:1–21 and Joshua 6:22–25 and read the backstory of Rahab.

Like Ruth, Rahab had not been born in Israel. Rahab was a Gentile prostitute living in Jericho prior to her conversion. Jericho was the first city conquered by Joshua when Israel came into the land of Canaan. Rahab believed in Israel's God and by faith hid Israel's spies when they entered Jericho to spy out the city.

Rahab helped the spies escape when she let them down by a rope through a window in her own house which had been built into the city wall. When Jericho was conquered by Israel, God spared her life and the lives of her family because of her faith and earlier courageous actions. Afterward, Rahab went to live in Israel and later married Salmon, who became the father of Boaz.

What does Rahab's story tell us about the heart of God?

Our God is a God of mercy, grace, and forgiveness. God looked beyond Rahab's sinfulness and saw her need. Rahab needed God, as we all do.

When Rahab put her faith in God, she was saved *"by grace through faith,"* (Ephesians 2:8–9). God honored her faith by allowing her to be in the lineage of His Son, Jesus Christ.

Our God is truly amazing!

There is nothing you have done or can do that our God will not forgive. Our God cares for the outcasts and invites us to eat at His table and to remain in His fields. There is safety, security, and stability in the refuge of God's wings. Rest in that truth today.

Verse of the Day:

Work out your own salvation

with fear and trembling,

for it is God who works in you,

both to will and to work

for his good pleasure.

Philippians 2:12~13

Day Five: New Hope
Ruth 2:17-23

Let's begin with prayer.

Slowly read or color-code Ruth 2:17–23.

Are you in the midst of a trial today where you feel like your hope is fading? Never lose your hope in God.

Worldly hope is a hope in something that might not happen. For example, we might *hope* to get a promotion or *hope* it doesn't rain on our picnic. This kind of hope is a desire for something good that we aren't certain will happen.

Biblical hope is a hope that is confident that good will come. We can expect it to happen just as God said it would.

Hope anchors our soul when our emotions are up and down. And while we are stuck in sorrow or suffering, God is always at work behind the scenes, plotting for our good and His glory. That's exactly what we will see in our reading today!

According to Ruth 2:17, how much grain had Ruth collected?

Ruth was strong! An ephah of barley would have been over one-half bushel, weighing about 30 to 40 pounds. She carried this all the way home, along with her leftovers from her dinner date!

Before she carried it all home, she worked late into the evening gleaning, then went to the threshing floor to pound out what she had gleaned so that it would be ready to use when she got home. Ruth is such a hard worker!

This was a large amount for one day of gleaning. God was generously providing for their needs, and Ruth was working hard to provide for Naomi's needs.

When Naomi saw the large amount of grain that Ruth had gleaned, what questions did Naomi ask, and what was Ruth's response?

Naomi offered a prayer of blessing over Boaz even before she realized Ruth had gleaned in his field saying, *"Blessed be the man who took notice of you."*

Ruth then told Naomi the man she had worked for was Boaz, and Naomi repeated her blessing.

Verse 20 is a pivotal point in our story because we begin to see a change in Naomi's heart and attitude. Naomi goes from being bitter and without hope to blessing and being filled with new hope.

Look at verse 20. What was the special relationship that Naomi and Ruth had with Boaz?

The anticipation of what Boaz could do for them filled Naomi with new hope. In Hebrew, the word for relative is *she'er* and is defined as body, flesh, and kindred by blood.

Boaz was a close blood relative. As a near blood relative, Boaz could fulfill the law of the kinsman-redeemer.

Read Leviticus 25:23–28 and 47–49. What were the responsibilities of the kinsman-redeemer?

In their culture, it was important to take care of your family, to provide for and protect them. A near relative could rescue relatives or "redeem" them.

In Hebrew, the word for redeem is *gaal*. It means to purchase and ransom, or redeemer and revenger.

A close relative could redeem a family member sold into slavery (Leviticus 25:47–49). Land that had been sold due to economic hardship could be bought back or redeemed so that it could be kept in the family (Leviticus 25:23–28).

Boaz could also redeem Ruth by fulfilling the levirate law by virtue of a levirate marriage, which we previously studied in Week Two, Day Three. If you remember, Deuteronomy 25:5–6 spoke of the brother's responsibility to marry his deceased brother's widow in order to conceive a son to carry on his brother's family name.

In the coming weeks, we will see how Boaz was a prophetic picture of Jesus Christ, our kinsman-redeemer.

The words of Boaz in verse 21 indicate how kind he was to Ruth and that he took a personal interest in her. He cared enough about her to protect her and provide for her needs.

How did Naomi caution Ruth in verse 22, and why?

It appears there was some danger present for the young women working in the fields. Not all field owners were as kind as Boaz; apparently, the women who gleaned in other fields were mistreated and even assaulted. Because of this, Naomi wanted Ruth to continue to enjoy the safety and security of gleaning in the fields of Boaz throughout the entire barley and wheat harvests, which was about a two-month period.

Ruth was loyal and obedient to Naomi's instructions and continued to glean in the fields of Boaz while living with her mother-in-law.

DISCUSSION QUESTIONS:

Just as Naomi experienced a turning point in her life, have you ever experienced a time in your own life when your bitterness was turned to faith and hope in God?

As we close out our study of chapter 2, what character traits do you admire in Boaz?

What character traits do you admire in Ruth?

". . .work out your own salvation with fear and trembling, for it is God who works in you, both to will and to work for his good pleasure." —Philippians 2:12b–13

As you work on developing your own Christian character, are there any traits that Boaz or Ruth possessed that need improvement in your own life?

Let's close out our week of study in prayer.

Dear Heavenly Father,

Thank you for being a kind and generous provider. Please help us to be humble, hospitable, gracious, merciful, and obedient to your word—as Boaz was. And make us like Ruth. Help us to be faithful, loyal, thoughtful, humble, respectful, gracious, selfless, hardworking, sacrificial, and obedient. We love you.

In Jesus' name we pray, Amen.

Week 4~Ruth 3:1~4:12

Verse of the Day:

Unless the LORD builds the house,

those who build it labor in vain.

Psalm 127:1

Day One: God's Plan
Ruth 3:1-4

Let's begin with prayer.

Slowly read or color-code Ruth 3:1–4.

This week's reading is very intense! I can't wait to dig into it with you!

In chapter 1, Naomi and Ruth returned from Moab to Bethlehem as widows to face a bleak future.

In chapter 2, we saw God sovereignly intervene in their lives when He brought a close relative, Boaz, to meet Ruth as she gleaned in his fields. Ruth and Boaz had their first date which was exciting to see, but the chapter ended on a low note. It closes with this line, "And she lived with her mother-in-law." (v.23)

Now chapter 3 is going to be exciting! All of it will take place during one night from sunset to sunrise. As our story continues to unfold, the scene changes from the fields of Boaz to the threshing floor. A period of time has gone by since Ruth first met Boaz and gleaned in his fields.

As a Jewish mother-in-law, Naomi felt responsible for Ruth's future. In 3:1, what duty did she seek to fulfill on behalf of Ruth, just as she'd earlier sought to do for her in Moab? (1:9)

In that day, it was customary for Jewish parents to arrange marriages for their children. Seeking "rest" for Ruth meant marriage, a husband, a family, and a home. In their culture, marriage provided security, safety, and a place of rest for a wife under the protective care of her husband.

Naomi's desire for Ruth to find rest in her husband, her family, and her home was admirable and Biblical.

DISCUSSION QUESTIONS:

Read Psalm 127 and 128. What does God say is needed to build a family and a home that is blessed by Him?

Notice that Boaz had initiated a relationship with Ruth. Back in his field, during the time of the wheat and barley harvest, he showed unusual kindness, care, and generosity towards Ruth.

Naomi knew God's Word regarding the role of a close relative or redeemer, and she began to make a plan. She now had hope in God's ability to provide for them through Boaz (Deuteronomy 25:5–6).

What did the Sadducees, first-century Jews, ask Jesus in Mathew 22:23–28 to indicate that they understood levirate marriage?

In the book of Matthew, a widow had been married to seven brothers, each of whom died shortly after they had married her. Their question was, whose wife would she be in heaven since all of them had been married to her. The Sadducees understood the widow had married each of the brothers in accordance with the levirate law.

According to Ruth 3:2, where did Naomi know Boaz would be that night, and what would he be doing?

Boaz would be "winnowing barley" at the threshing floor. Winnowing barley is tossing the grain into the air to separate the grain from the chaff. Then the grain would be gathered up to be sold or put into storage. Boaz would have worked late and then slept all night at the threshing floor to guard his grain against theft (3:7).

Observing 3:3, how did Naomi instruct Ruth to prepare herself to meet Boaz at the threshing floor that evening?

First, Ruth was told to "wash" herself. In other words, take a bath. Then Ruth was to "anoint" herself with a fragrant perfume or oils so that she would smell good. Next, Ruth was told to put on her "cloak," which could be interpreted to mean different things. It could mean that Ruth should change her clothes and put on one of her finer garments. Or because Ruth was a widow, she may have needed to remove her mourning clothes and dress in something reserved for a more festive occasion.

Generally, a "cloak" was a larger, outer garment. If this is the interpretation, then Ruth would have been able to hide her identity from Boaz since Naomi instructed her not to make her presence known to Boaz until he had finished eating and drinking.

We can conclude from verse 3 that there was a meal following the winnowing of the barley. Again, we see the humility of Boaz as he worked, ate, and drank right alongside his servants.

Look at 3:4. What was Ruth to do next?

Oh, boy! Here's where it gets a little dicey! This is not a typical Bible story. There is no way to escape the overtones of this passage when Naomi uses words like "uncover" and "lie down." But Ruth was proposing marriage to Boaz according to the levirate law, so she was doing nothing improper by following Naomi's instructions. A widow could go to the nearest relative and ask him to marry her.

It is obvious that Naomi had trust in the godly character of Boaz, or she would not have instructed Ruth to go to the threshing floor that night.

And it's important to note that Naomi told her to observe the place where Boaz lies down. Basically, Naomi is saying, do not get this wrong Ruth!

Finally, Ruth was to go, uncover his feet, and place herself at his feet, signifying to him that she was offering herself to her redeemer, Boaz.

And we'll pause the story right here until tomorrow.

But in conclusion, turn back to Genesis 19:30–38. Read the story of Lot and his two daughters. Take note of how similar this story is to Ruth's. There are two women plotting to preserve their family line, only that time sin was involved. What was the firstborn son named according to verse 37?

Jewish readers would have known the history of the Moabites and been able to connect the similarities of these two stories. But the main difference between these two stories is the character and faith of the women. Lot's daughters devised a plan that was not obedient to God, but Ruth and Naomi devised a plan that *was* obedient to God.

Are you trusting God today for whatever hopes and dreams that you have?

Do not step outside of God's will to devise your own plan.

"Be patient and wait on the Lord." —Psalm 37:7

Trust Him to take care of you.

He loves you so.

Verse of the Day:

All Scripture is breathed out by

God and profitable for teaching,

for reproof, for correction,

and for training in righteousness.

2 Timothy 3:16

Day Two: Ruth's Courage
Ruth 3:5-9

Let's begin with prayer.

Slowly read or color-code Ruth 3:5–9.

As we begin today's reading, I can feel the tension rising. Everything Ruth is about to do takes courage.

Ruth is taking her bath, putting on her perfume, and getting dressed in her cloak. I can't imagine what the walk across the field must have felt like as she headed towards the threshing floor.

Ruth is about to take the biggest risk of her life and follow the instructions of Naomi. She is going to hide out and watch Boaz as he eats and drinks. I am sure her heart was beating fast as she admired him from afar, watching and waiting—waiting on Boaz not only to lie down, but also to fall asleep.

Let's see what happens next.

What was Ruth's response to Naomi's instructions in verses 5 and 6?

Ruth was fully obedient. Verse 6 says that Ruth acted upon Naomi's instructions and "did just as her mother-in-law had commanded her."

How was this courageous of Ruth? What risks were involved that might have caused her to disobey Naomi?

Ruth could have been considered too bold in initiating a marriage proposal to Boaz. Boaz could have rejected her and shamed her. Her reputation as a godly woman could have been damaged. Her obedience required courage.

What does Ruth's full obedience tell you about her relationship with Naomi?

Ruth loved, respected, honored, and trusted her mother-in-law. She understood that Naomi knew God's Word and that asking Boaz to redeem her was the right thing to do.

DISCUSSION QUESTIONS:

What do we learn about God's Word in 2 Timothy 3:16–17? How does Scripture provide teaching and training for godly living?

Since Scripture is divinely inspired, we should know it and seek to obey it.

Like Ruth, are you willing to take godly, Biblical instruction from others? Why or why not?

Read Ruth 3:7. What does Ruth do next?

Remember, Israel had recently experienced a famine, but now there was a full harvest, so winnowing the harvest was a time of celebration, which included eating and drinking. The heart of Boaz was "merry." He was joyful and had a sense of well-being because God had blessed him with a bountiful harvest.

Ruth observed where Boaz went to lie down to rest. Then, obeying Naomi's instructions, she came softly, uncovered his feet (a ceremonial act that was completely proper) and put herself at the feet of Boaz knowing that he could redeem her.

According to verse 8, when Boaz woke up at midnight, what did he find?

Remember, Boaz was sleeping with his grain to protect it from being stolen. So imagine how shocked he must have been to wake up and find someone so close to him.

In verse 9, Boaz asked the woman, "Who are you?" How did Ruth answer his question?

Many times we have seen her identified in the book of Ruth as "Ruth, the Moabite," but here Ruth identified herself as the "servant" of Boaz.

After identifying herself to Boaz, what did Ruth specifically ask Boaz to do and why?

Once again, she refers to herself as the servant of Boaz. Remember, Ruth was the widow of Mahlon, the oldest son of Elimelech, who died without children. Ruth was calling Boaz to attend to his responsibility as her redeemer, to redeem her family and her land.

In Ruth 2:12, Ruth had put herself under the wings of the Lord, the God of Israel. Now she was asking to be put under the wings of Boaz as a husband to her. This is a beautiful picture of marriage.

To better understand this, let's read Ezekiel 16:8:

"When I passed by you again and saw you, behold, you were at the age for love, and I spread the corner of my garment over you and covered your nakedness; I made my vow to you and entered into a covenant with you declares the Lord God, and you became mine."

God is speaking allegorically of His relationship with Israel. Spreading one's skirt or garment over a person was a symbolic act that showed you were claiming that person for yourself. Here the Lord spoke of spreading the corner of His garment over Israel, indicating that He had entered into a covenant with Israel to become her husband. He took Israel as His own.

I love the final three words of this verse, *"you became mine."* If you are married, then you know what it's like to have your husband become yours and for you to become his.

Isn't this what we all long for, to be seen and known and loved. We want someone to choose us.

Look what 1 Peter 2:9 says about us!

"But you are a chosen people, a royal priesthood, a holy nation, a people for his own possession, that you may proclaim the excellencies of him who called you out of darkness into his marvelous light." —1 Peter 2:9

Whether you are married or single, God has chosen you! You are His and He is yours, and you are deeply loved.

May we rest in the security and protection of our Heavenly Father as we live courageously like Ruth.

Verse of the Day:

"Wait for the LORD; be strong,

and let your heart take courage;

wait for the LORD!"

Psalm 27:14

Day Three: Waiting on God
Ruth 3:10-18

Begin with prayer.

Slowly read or color-code Ruth 3:10–18.

Today we will complete our study in chapter 3, and I can already hear wedding bells starting to ring! At the end of the chapter, we will see Ruth, Naomi, and Boaz all waiting on God to settle the matter as to whom Ruth would marry. These will be the final words of Ruth and Naomi as they do not speak again in this book.

Let's look at verse 10.

What was the reaction of Boaz to Ruth's proposal of marriage? Did Boaz understand her request?

Boaz seemed pleased by Ruth's request to redeem and marry her. In verse 10, he praised her for her kindness and offered a blessing over her as he'd done earlier in 2:12.

He again referred to Ruth as "my daughter" which indicates the difference in their ages. This was made clear when Boaz praised her for not going after young men, whether poor or rich, but honorably desiring instead to be married to the older Boaz.

In verse 10, Boaz commended Ruth, saying, "this last kindness is greater than the first." What do you think that statement meant?

Ruth's decision to serve Naomi, her mother-in-law, was her "first" kindness, and the "last" kindness was greater, her desire to serve Boaz in the future as his wife.

In verse 11, Boaz calmed Ruth's fears. What did Boaz promise her and why?

Boaz promised Ruth that he would do all that she had asked of him because it was known by all of the people of Bethlehem that Ruth was a "worthy woman." Ruth was a woman of excellence, possessing a noble and virtuous character.

It is interesting to note that 2:1 uses the same definition for Boaz, calling him "a worthy man."

Boaz and Ruth were perfectly matched.

He was a "worthy man," and she was a "worthy woman."

DISCUSSION QUESTIONS:

Proverbs 31:10–31 describes the virtuous woman. Read these verses and compare your character and actions to the woman described in Proverbs 31. Are there any character traits you need to work on?

As women, we need to remember that God loves us. Every woman who fears the Lord and walks humbly and obediently with her God is a "worthy woman."

Let's pray that God will help us to grow in our love for Him as well as serving those God brings into our lives. And may all we do glorify Him because He is worthy.

"Worthy are you, our Lord and God, to receive glory and honor and power." —Revelation 4:11

According to verse 12, before Boaz could redeem Ruth, there was one problem. What was the problem?

The wedding bells just stopped! There is one problem. There was another redeemer, a nearer relative than Boaz. This relative would have a claim to Ruth and the estate of Elimelech before Boaz.

We wonder if Naomi was aware of this nearer relative that could be a redeemer. Scripture doesn't tell us.

Because Boaz was a righteous man, he respected and put this man's rights before his own. Boaz would need to talk to this nearer relative in the morning.

According to verse 13, if the nearer relative was unwilling to redeem Ruth, what promise or pledge did Boaz make to Ruth?

The phrase "as the Lord lives" is the most solemn, binding oath a Jew could vow. Boaz promised that he would care for Ruth and Naomi if the nearer relative was not willing to redeem Naomi's land and marry Ruth.

According to verses 14–17, how did Boaz demonstrate his integrity and righteous character?

Boaz was protecting Ruth's reputation as well as his own. He did not want to give anyone an opportunity to form a wrong opinion or gossip about Ruth.

As Ruth was leaving, Boaz showed his generosity and kindness to her by gifting her with six measures of barley to be given to her mother-in-law. Boaz did not want Ruth to return to Naomi empty-handed. Possibly this was his way of showing that he did indeed plan to honor his promise to care for them should the nearer redeemer decline to do so.

After Ruth shared with Naomi all that had happened and the promise Boaz had made to her, what was Naomi's advice to Ruth in verse 18?

Naomi told Ruth to "wait" for Boaz to carry out his promise to her. Naomi was well aware of the righteousness of Boaz and also that he was a man of action. She assured Ruth that Boaz would not rest until the matter was settled that day.

And so this chapter closes with a sense of anticipation because Naomi knew that whoever redeemed Ruth—whether Boaz or the nearer relative—that day would be Ruth's day of redemption!

It is interesting to note in Ruth 3:3 that Naomi counseled Ruth to "go" down to the threshing floor that night, but in verse 18, Naomi's counsel was to "wait." They had acted. They had done all they could do. Now Ruth must patiently wait on the Lord to work through Boaz before she could see how this matter would turn out.

This implies that there is a time to act and a time to wait. What does Ecclesiastes 3:1–8 tell us?

Ecclesiastes 3:1 states that there is a time for every matter under heaven. For everything there is a season, a proper time to act and a proper time to wait. Every event happens in its time.

Are you currently in God's waiting room, waiting for God to answer your prayers? How difficult is waiting on God for you?

David said in Psalm 27:14, *"Wait for the LORD; be strong, and let your heart take courage; wait for the LORD!"*

Whatever you are waiting for today, persevere.

Be strong.

Have courage.

Do not get ahead of God, but rather, wait for the Lord. He loves you!

Verse of the Day:

Do not be anxious about tomorrow,

for tomorrow will be anxious for itself.

Sufficient for the day is its own trouble.

Matthew 6:34

Day Four: A Sigh of Relief
Ruth 4:1-6

Begin with prayer.

Slowly read or color-code Ruth 4:1–6.

It's time to begin the fourth and final chapter of Ruth. The second chapter was just a day in Ruth's life, and the third chapter was a night in Ruth's life, but this chapter is going to catapult us all the way through time—to King David!

Having studied the first three chapters of Ruth, we have seen how God has sovereignly moved to bring Naomi and Ruth and Ruth and Boaz together.

As we left Ruth and Boaz at the end of chapter 3, they are in love and want to get married. Ruth was patiently waiting on the Lord to work through Boaz to see if either he or a nearer relative to Elimelech was willing to redeem her. Boaz had already promised Ruth that he would be willing to redeem her land and marry her if the nearer relative declined to do so.

Chapter 4 will bring this amazing love story to a beautiful conclusion. If you are the type who enjoys happy endings, you will not be disappointed!

The theme of chapter 4 is redemption.

You will notice that some form of this word—*redeem*, *redeemer*, or *redemption*—is repeated 13 times in the ESV, making it a very important keyword. The Hebrew word translated redeem is *ga'al*, and the definition of the word is to be the next of kin (and as such to buy back a relative's property, marry his widow, etc.), avenger, purchase, ransom, redeemer, or revenger.

However, there can be no redemption unless the kinsman/relative is willing and able to pay the price of redemption. Also, no one was obligated to take the role of kinsman-redeemer. He did have a choice in the matter.

Boaz had spent the previous night at the threshing floor. According to verse 1, where did Boaz immediately go the next morning?

Since Boaz went "up," the threshing floor must have been below the level of the city gate.

In ancient Israel, the city gate was the public meeting place where civic affairs, personal business, and official legal transactions occurred in the presence of witnesses. Verse 1 tells us that the nearer relative came by the gate (another indication to us of God's sovereignty), and Boaz respectfully called him "friend" and asked him to sit down, which he did.

Most likely Boaz was anxious to find out if this nearer relative, who by the law of redemption and the law of levirate marriage, was willing to accept the responsibility of the kinsman-redeemer. Boaz and this nearer relative were not brothers to Mahlon, but it appears that it was legal to extend the scope of levirate marriage to include the nearest relative. Some believe that this nearer relative could have been the older brother of Boaz or possibly a cousin.

Before a legal transaction took place, whom did Boaz ask to serve as witnesses between him and the nearer relative in verse 2?

Boaz called for ten of Bethlehem's older leaders who sat in the city gate to witness their legal transaction. We do not know why he chose ten elders, unless ten elders comprised a full court. Some commentators think that Boaz himself may have been one of the elders of the city.

Boaz was anxious to determine if this nearer relative was willing to fulfill his duties. In verses 3–4, how did Boaz describe the situation to him, and what was the nearer relative's initial response?

Boaz was smart. He knew that most men are interested in acquiring more property, especially to keep it in the family line. So he only informed him that the widow Naomi was about to sell the parcel of land that belonged to her deceased husband and their relative Elimelech.

The property must have been valuable because the nearer relative immediately was interested in buying it.

Then Boaz surprises this man with a package deal that includes Ruth, the Moabite. If a son was born of their union, the property would eventually belong to their first-born son in order to preserve the family name of Elimelech and Mahlon.

In verse 6, how did the nearer relative respond to this information?

And we all breathe a collective sigh of relief.

Boaz is finally able to become Ruth's knight in shining armor!

In verse 6, what reason did the nearer relative give for refusing to redeem the land and marry Ruth?

We can only speculate that he may already have been married and had a son or sons. The division of the land and inheritance would have been detrimental to them because he would have to split it between his present sons and any son he may have in the future with Ruth.

DISCUSSION QUESTIONS:

Are you a worrier?

As we study the book of Ruth, I am amazed at how calm Ruth is. Ruth does not worry about leaving her home in Moab. She is at peace. She does not worry about where her next meal will come from. She works hard. Ruth does not give way to fear when she is told to go to Boaz at night. She does as she is instructed. And Ruth seems to be completely at peace waiting on Boaz to go to the nearer kinsman.

Ruth's life had been riddled with stress. The death of a husband, poverty, a large move to a new country, and hard labor were just some of what she faced, but Ruth's trust in God is revealed through her ability to put one foot in front of the other and do the next hard thing.

Is there something in your life today that you are worried about? What is the next hard thing that you need to do?

How does watching Ruth's strength as she waits on the Lord to sovereignly work things out in her life encourage you?

In Matthew 6:34 Jesus said to us, *"Do not be anxious about tomorrow, for tomorrow will be anxious for itself. Sufficient for the day is its own trouble."* —Matthew 6:34

When stress and the unknown press in and fear rears its ugly head, we are all tempted to worry. But worrying accomplishes nothing. Jesus wants us to trust in Him and His good plan for us.

If you are going through a dark time in your life, remember that your story is not over yet. Like our story in Ruth, God is not finished! There is so much more to come. There is always hope with Jesus!

Turn your worry into prayer. God is with you, and He loves you

Verse of the Day:

Children are a heritage from the LORD,

the fruit of the womb a reward.

Psalm 127:3

Day Five: Boaz Redeems Ruth
Ruth 4:7-12

Begin with prayer.

Slowly read or color-code Ruth 4:7–12.

This is the moment we have all been waiting for! Ruth is about to go from being a foreigner, a Moabite, a servant, and a widow, to becoming Boaz's wife!

In Israel, in former times, a legal transaction was finalized not by signing a written agreement, but by a symbolic or ceremonial act that others witnessed. What was the ancient custom that was used to confirm a legal transaction? (verses 7–8)

The transfer of the sandal from one man to another symbolized the transaction agreement was complete and final between them. Verse 8 tells us the redeemer (the nearer relative) removed and gave his sandal to Boaz and said to him regarding the land, "Buy it for yourself." The nearer relative was legally surrendering and transferring his right to the land to Boaz. We hear no more about this redeemer in Scripture after he gives his sandal to Boaz.

A similar custom is recorded in Deuteronomy 25:5–10 involving a different situation. What did you learn about the removal of a sandal from this passage of Scripture?

These verses are speaking of levirate marriage. Though a brother-in-law was not compelled to marry his brother's widow, it was strongly encouraged. If he refused to marry her in order to carry on his brother's name in Israel, the widow in the presence of the elders could shame him publicly by pulling off his sandal and spitting in his face.

Returning to Ruth, once the nearer redeemer surrendered his rights, Boaz immediately accepted the responsibility to legally buy and redeem all the land that belonged to Naomi's husband, Elimelech, and her two sons, Chilion and Mahlon, Ruth's deceased husband.

How then was Boaz Ruth's kinsman-redeemer in verse 10?

Boaz kept his promise to Ruth to redeem her. Boaz bought Ruth to be his wife.

In fulfilling his duties as the kinsman-redeemer, what else was Boaz willing to do?

Boaz would preserve the family name of the dead so that his name would not be cut off and forgotten. Boaz would raise a son to continue the name of Elimelech and Mahlon. This was a very important part of the law of levirate marriage.

In verse 11, who willingly witnessed the redemption transaction and gave their strong approval?

The ten elders and all the people at the Bethlehem gate testified that the land and Ruth had been bought and redeemed by Boaz.

Then the elders and witnesses also further showed their approval by giving a public prayer of blessing upon their marriage. Their prayer was comprised of three separate requests, one for each member of their future family: Ruth, Boaz and any children that the Lord would give to them.

In verse 11, what was their prayer request for Ruth?

Rachel and Leah were the wives of Jacob, and each of them had sons. Rachel had two sons, and Leah had six sons. Rachel gave her servant, Bilhah, and Leah gave her servant, Zilpah, to become Jacob's concubines. They each had two sons. These 12 sons of Jacob became the 12 tribes which formed the nation of Israel (Genesis 35:22b–26).

So the people were requesting that the Lord bless Ruth and Boaz with many children. Rachel and Leah built up the house of Israel. Ruth, too, would build up the house of Israel as King David and Jesus would come through her lineage!

In verse 11, what was their prayer request for Boaz?

Remember, Ephrathah is another name for Bethlehem (Micah 5:2), the city in which our Savior Jesus was born. The elders and the people desired that Boaz would continue to be virtuous (2:1), prominent, and influential in Bethlehem.

In verse 12, what was their prayer request regarding future offspring/children?

As you can see, prosperity in marriage was measured in terms of children. Offspring guaranteed the permanence of your family line. Boaz and Ruth's first-born son would be considered the son of Mahlon, but any additional sons would legally be the offspring of Boaz.

In observing verses 11–12, where are children acknowledged to come from?

In verse 11, the people request that the Lord make Ruth fertile, and in verse 12, it says that the Lord is the one who gives offspring or children to build a family.

In Israel, children were considered a blessing and a gift from the Lord.

Psalm 127:3 says, *"Behold, children are a heritage from the LORD, the fruit of the womb a reward."*

What are your thoughts about children? Do you consider them a blessing or a burden? How are children viewed in our society?

Many adults do view children as great blessings and gifts from God and love them dearly. But sadly, some do not. This is revealed by the number of children who are neglected, abused, seen as an inconvenience, or aborted.

What did Jesus teach about the value of children in Luke 18:15–17?

During His earthly ministry, Jesus was never too busy for the children. Children possess a childlike faith and humility that is required to enter the kingdom of heaven. Jesus used the children as an example to encourage adults to become more like children if they want to enter the kingdom of heaven.

In Ruth 4:12, Perez, who is a direct ancestor to Boaz, is mentioned. You can read the story of the birth of Perez to Tamar and Judah in Genesis 38:1–30. Tamar became pregnant with twins by her father-in-law, Judah. The son that was born first was Perez. As you read through Genesis 38, you will see the levirate connection.

DISCUSSION QUESTIONS:

What can we learn from this passage of Scripture about marriage, the family, and prayer?

Biblical marriage is a sacred covenant between a man and a woman designed by God. God intended for marriage to be a lifelong union (Genesis 2:24). Therefore, we should bless and pray over one another's marriages and families. Today, it is especially important to pray because our Christian marriages and families are under attack from Satan and the culture we live in.

Family life can get messy when a spouse or child decides to rebel against God. If your family has been under attack lately, go to God and ask Him for help. Seek out an older woman, a pastor, or a counselor for support. You do not have to walk this road alone, and you are not alone. So many are silently wrestling with similar struggles. God has given us the church, the family of God, to be there for each other and support each other.

There are great blessings when God is at the center of your family. God gets all the glory, and our marriages and families are a testimony and a witness to others. Even in the midst of our struggles, we can walk in faith and be a light.

Please write out a prayer for your family and commit to pray daily for each of them, including yourself. As we pray, our prayers will draw us not only closer to God, but also to one another.

Week 5~Ruth 4:13~22 and

A Study of the Kinsman~Redeemer

Verse of the Day:

Blessed be the LORD,

who has not left you this day

without a redeemer.

Ruth 4:14

Day 1: A Wedding, A Baby, and a Lineage
Ruth 4:13-22

Begin with prayer.

Slowly read or color-code Ruth 4:13–22.

We have read three chapters filled with details leading up to the events that all of us have been waiting for—a wedding and a baby! And just like that, in one short verse, it's over, and we move on.

But let's not gloss over this. Wedding celebrations during the time of the judges often lasted for seven days. Samson was a judge in Israel, and his wedding celebration in Timnah lasted seven days (Judges 14:10–18). So they definitely had the time of their lives rejoicing in their marriage! I wish our weddings were still that long. How fun!

But this is about more than a love story. During the darkest of times, our God was providing something greater—a greater love story. Let's take a look.

In verse 13, after the marriage of Boaz and Ruth, how was the prayer of blessing given by the people and the elders fulfilled?

Boaz "went in" to Ruth. This is the Old Testament's way of saying that they consummated their marriage. "The Lord gave her conception." The Lord blessed their union with a male child, a son, Mahlon's long-awaited legal heir.

In Moab, Ruth had been married to Mahlon, but they had no children. Now God has rewarded her faithful obedience to Him with a son.

If you remember, in Ruth 1:20–21, the women of Bethlehem had witnessed Naomi's return from Moab. They had heard of her emptiness, bitterness, and despair. But now in Ruth 4, Naomi is no longer empty, but full because of the birth of her grandson. The Lord had restored Naomi's hope.

What joyful blessing did the women of Bethlehem express to Naomi in 4:14?

The women in Bethlehem shared in the joy of this newborn baby boy. They praised God and said, "Blessed be the Lord, who has not left you this day without a redeemer." In this verse, this is a reference to the baby, not his father, Boaz.

Just as the people and the elders had prayed that the name of Boaz would be "renowned" (prominent and influential) in Bethlehem (v.11), the women now requested that Naomi's grandson's name also be "renowned" in Israel.

In verse 15, what more do the women say to Naomi about her newborn grandson?

This grandchild is going to be a source of blessing in Naomi's life. He will renew within Naomi a sense of joy and hope, and this grandson will care for Naomi in her later years. He will be her provider and protector, keeping her safe and secure.

If you are a grandparent, share how your grandchildren have blessed you, brought joy into your life, and given you hope for the future.

In verse 15, how did the women give high praise to Ruth? What did they say to Naomi about her daughter-in-law?

The women recognized the great love that Ruth had for Naomi. It is interesting to note that this is the only use of the word love in the entire book of Ruth! It is speaking of the love that a daughter-in-law had for her mother-in-law.

The women praised and honored Ruth by telling Naomi that even if she'd given birth to seven sons, Ruth was of more value and worth to her. The number seven represents perfection in the Bible. Having seven sons symbolized the supreme blessing that could come to a Jewish family (Job 1:2).

The women were saying that they held Ruth in high esteem because she had exceeded that standard. Ruth's love for Naomi was equal to or better than that of seven sons.

It is also interesting to note that in Ruth 1:21, Naomi said she "went away full, and the Lord has brought me back empty." Naomi forgot to mention that she had Ruth with her when she returned to Bethlehem from Moab. Because of the selfless love and loyalty of Ruth, Naomi now had been restored to fullness with the birth of a son to Ruth.

DISCUSSION QUESTIONS:

What lessons can we learn from Ruth? How is Ruth's love, loyalty, and care for her aging mother-in-law a model for us to follow?

Ruth was humble, gracious, self-sacrificing, gentle yet strong, kind, respectful, and obedient in the way she faithfully honored, loved, cared, and provided for Naomi. If you think about it, Ruth now actually had two mothers-in-law. She had her Jewish mother-in-law, Naomi, and she had her Gentile mother-in-law, Rahab, the mother of Boaz!

Verse 16 tells us that Naomi held this baby boy in her arms and took over his care as a godly grandmother does for her little grandson. What was the baby named, and who named him? (verse 17)

In Biblical times, names had meanings. Obed in Hebrew is "Owbed," and means serving. Obed would serve Naomi. This is the only place in the Old Testament where someone other than the immediate family named a child.

The neighborhood women also said, "A son has been born to Naomi." In Hebrew, the word "son" often means descendant, and here actually refers to a grandson. Ruth had given birth to Obed, but he was Naomi's "son" because of the levirate obligation.

And so this chapter closes with Naomi holding the child in her lap.

She came to Bethlehem empty, but now her hands are full. Wow! That's our God!

What do you learn from the genealogy recorded at the end of chapter 4?

God rewarded Ruth and Boaz with a son, Obed, who would become the grandfather of King David, the King of Israel who was a man after God's own heart. This meant that Ruth and Boaz would be the great-grandparents of King David.

How did God further honor and reward Ruth and Boaz? In whose genealogy do you also find them according to Matthew 1:1–16?

Ruth and Boaz were not only in the lineage of the King of Israel, David, but also in the lineage of Israel's Messiah and God's only son, the Lord Jesus Christ.

In Luke 2:1–7, we read about Mary and Joseph traveling to their family's hometown for a census. That hometown was the hometown of Boaz, Bethlehem, and the city of David. And there in Bethlehem, Jesus was born.

Isn't that amazing how it all ties together! The story of Ruth and Boaz is about so much more than just Ruth and Boaz.

Boaz and Ruth's names will be remembered through all generations because of their faithful obedience to God and because of God's faithful, loving, and gracious care for His people. He sovereignly accomplished His divine plan to bring His Son into the world.

Praise God!

Jesus Christ is the ultimate Redeemer that came into the world giving hope to all mankind. Like Naomi and Ruth, we too have a kinsman-redeemer, and His name is Jesus Christ.

Let's continue with our study to see how Jesus fulfilled the duties of His role as our kinsman-redeemer. It is going to be so good!

Verse of the Day:

You are not your own,

for you were bought with a price.

So glorify God in your body.

1 Corinthians 6:20

Day 2: Jesus Christ, Our Kinsman-Redeemer

Begin with prayer.

During the first week of our study together, I mentioned my high school English class and how I needed the class discussions to draw out the symbolism in a story. Today I am excited to begin an in-depth look at the symbolism that is woven throughout the book of Ruth. This is beyond exciting to me, especially because it is so personal. While I have grown very fond of Ruth and Boaz, it is the God of Ruth and Boaz that I deeply love. Learning more about how God loves me is so comforting.

1 Corinthians 6:19–20 says, *"Do you not know that your body is a temple of the Holy Spirit within you, whom you have from God? You are not your own, for you were bought with a price. So glorify God in your body."*

Friends, Satan longs to own you, but he did not buy you. He can't have you. You were bought with the price of Jesus' blood. You are God's! You belong to Him, and He belongs to you. Let's take a deeper look at this truth in the book of Ruth.

Let's begin with a brief review of the duties of the kinsman-redeemer:

1) The kinsman-redeemer had to be a close blood relative.

Look at Ruth 2:1.

Was Boaz a close blood relative? Yes or No (circle one)

2) He was to redeem the land (Leviticus 25:25).

Look at Ruth 4:9.

Did Boaz redeem the land? Yes or No

3) He was to redeem a blood relative from slavery if they had become so poor that they had sold themselves into slavery, which was a common occurrence in ancient Bible times (Leviticus 25:47–49).

Look at Ruth 4:10.

Did Boaz buy Ruth? Yes or No

4) He must be willing to redeem (Ruth 4:3–6).

Look at Ruth 3:9–13.

Was Boaz willing to redeem Ruth? Yes or No

A nearer relative, closer than Boaz, was not willing to redeem both the land and Ruth (Ruth 4:3–6).

5) He must be able to pay the redemption price (Ruth 4:9–10).

Look at Ruth 4:9–10.

Was Boaz able to pay the redemption price? Yes or No

6) There is one additional duty we have not yet studied. *A kinsman-redeemer was also the "avenger of blood."*

A kinsman-redeemer was to avenge the murder of a close, blood relative. Blood avengers were appointed to kill only a murderer of a close relative, not one who had unintentionally killed a relative. One who committed an unintentional murder could flee to a city of refuge for protection from the blood avenger (Numbers 35:9–21).

Israel was instructed by God that the shedding of innocent blood was always to be avenged. The Biblical penalty for murder was capital punishment instituted by God in Genesis 9:5–6.

So far we have reviewed the duties of the kinsman-redeemer, and we have seen the picture that Boaz provided of our kinsman-redeemer, Jesus Christ.

Now let's look at the best part—Jesus and His love for us!

Look back at the list of qualifications. What was the first qualification Jesus had to fulfill in order to redeem us?

Read John 1:1–2 and 14. How did Jesus fulfill the first qualification of being a close, blood relative?

When Jesus, who is God, became a man, He fulfilled the requirement and fully qualified to become our Redeemer.

Read Luke 1:30–35 and Galatians 4:4. What do you learn about the supernatural birth of Jesus?

The Holy Spirit came upon Mary, who was a virgin, and she conceived a son. God is His Father. Mary gave birth to a flesh and blood baby boy, the Son of the Most High God. Jesus did not cease to be God when He took on humanity. Jesus is fully God and fully man.

DISCUSSION QUESTIONS:

How does it make you feel to know that Jesus Christ was willing to leave the glories of heaven to come to earth and take on the form of a man?

You are so loved and valued!

What a great sacrifice Jesus was willing to make on our behalf.

The story of Ruth and Boaz is one of the most beautiful examples of God's love and sovereignty recorded in the Bible. The redemption and the relationship between Boaz and Ruth help us to have a deeper understanding of our own redemption and relationship with Jesus Christ.

Just as Boaz became Ruth's kinsman-redeemer and redeemed his Gentile bride, so Jesus Christ, our kinsman-redeemer, will redeem His own Gentile bride, the church.

Jesus is our Bridegroom, and we are His bride. Someday our Bridegroom will come to claim us. He will take us to be with Him forever, and we will celebrate the marriage supper of the Lamb (Revelation 19:7).

In light of this truth, may we rejoice and give God praise as we are *"waiting for our blessed hope, the appearing of the glory of our great God and Savior Jesus Christ."* —Titus 2:13

Verse of the Day:

"Worthy is the Lamb who was slain,

to receive power and wealth and wisdom

and might and honor and glory and blessing!"

Revelation 5:12

Day 3: Worthy Is the Lamb!

Begin with prayer.

Yesterday we looked at the first qualification of a kinsman-redeemer and how Jesus fulfilled that qualification. Today we'll look at the second qualification.

Do you remember when Boaz went to the nearer kinsman and offered the land and Ruth to him? That man turned down the offer. Do you remember that man's name?

He is unnamed.

Forever his name is forgotten. He was unwilling to make the sacrifice to purchase the land that included Ruth and Naomi.

But Boaz was willing!

No matter the cost and no matter how it affected his reputation, Boaz was willing to make sacrifices to take on Ruth and Naomi and their land. In the same way, Jesus is willing to redeem us, no matter the cost!

Romans 5:6–8 says, "*For while we were still weak, at the right time Christ died for the ungodly.*

For one will scarcely die for a righteous person—though perhaps for a good person one would dare even to die—but God shows his love for us in that while we were still sinners, Christ died for us."

The love that Jesus has for us is a deep sacrificial love. You are so loved!

Let's take a look at the second qualification of a kinsman-redeemer.

Turn back to your lesson from yesterday. What was the second qualification?

Now read Genesis 1:1 and 26–28. Who does the earth belong to, and who was to have dominion or rule over it?

The earth belongs to the Lord because God created the heavens and the earth and all that is in it, but God gave man the responsibility to rule over the earth.

Read Genesis 3:1–7, 22–24, and Romans 5:12. A battle began in the Garden of Eden. Who entered the garden bringing sin and death with him, and what were the consequences of man's disobedience?

The serpent, a manifestation of Satan (Revelation 12:9), entered the garden and tempted the woman to sin by eating of the forbidden fruit of the tree of the knowledge of good and evil. Eve ate and gave it to Adam who also ate of the fruit. It was at this point that man fell, and sin and death entered the world.

God drove Adam and Eve out of the Garden of Eden because of their sinfulness.

What do you learn in 1 John 5:19? Who presently rules over the earth?

We know that the earth does not rightfully belong to Satan, but to the Lord who created it.

Read Revelation 5:1–14. We will look at this in more detail later in our study, but in the future, who is going to redeem the earth and take it back from Satan?

It is believed that the sealed scroll in Revelation, taken from the hand of God by the Lion of the tribe of Judah (the Lamb of God slain from the foundation of the world), represents the title deed to the earth.

Jesus Christ is the only one who is worthy to take the scroll, redeem the earth, and take back what was lost under Adam. This will put an end to Satan's rule over the earth. Jesus will redeem the earth and rule and reign over it.

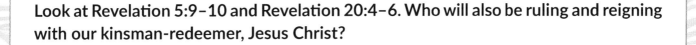

Look at Revelation 5:9–10 and Revelation 20:4–6. Who will also be ruling and reigning with our kinsman-redeemer, Jesus Christ?

Believers will rule and reign with Christ as God had originally intended for them to do. We will receive back what was lost under Adam.

DISCUSSION QUESTIONS:

Is your heart leaping right now at all of these connections between Ruth and Boaz and Jesus and us? Share what you are feeling and how God is speaking directly to you through His Word.

I hope today's reading has filled you to the brim with hope! I am simply in awe of how God has orchestrated this picture of His deep love for us.

Praise His holy name!

"Worthy is the Lamb who was slain, to receive power and wealth and wisdom and might and honor and glory and blessing!" —Revelation 5:12

Verse of the Day:

Thanks be to God for his inexpressible gift!

2 Corinthians 9:15

Day 4: A Great Gift!

Begin with prayer.

In chapter one, Ruth and Naomi were facing the worst days of their lives. They could not have known how God was setting the stage for their greatest blessings to come. In the same way, in our darkest moments, we cannot see what is up ahead, but we have a sovereign God who is at work in our lives for our good and His glory.

Naomi and Ruth chose to trust God with their lives, and as a result, He blessed them. We too need to trust God even in the hard times, because we have a Redeemer who loves us and wants to bless us too.

Let's take a deeper look at the next three qualifications for the kinsman-redeemer.

Turn back to your lesson from Day Two of this week. What is the third qualification?

In our earlier studies, we saw that redemption can mean to set free by paying a price. It also means to purchase or ransom.

Read John 8:34, Romans 3:23, Romans 6:16, and 2 Peter 2:19. How have we been enslaved? What are we slaves to?

Spiritually, all of us are in bondage to sin and to Satan. We cannot set ourselves free from the power of sin, the penalty of sin, or the presence of sin in our lives.

Look at Acts 4:11–12 and John 8:34–36. Who alone can provide freedom and redemption to us from our sins?

The only one who can set us free from our sins is Jesus, so we must put our faith in Him. He alone has the power to save and redeem us.

Look back at Day Two and write out the fourth qualification below.

What do you learn from the following verses: Mark 10:45, Luke 22:39–46, John 1:29, John 10:14–18, Ephesians 1:7, Philippians 2:5–11, and Revelation 5:9? What was the redemption price, and was Jesus willing to pay it to redeem us?

Jesus humbly and willingly laid down His life for us when He shed His blood and died on the cross. He gave His life as a ransom for many and purchased us from the slave market of sin to set us free to serve the living God.

Flip back to Day Two one last time. What is the fifth qualification?

Look up Hebrews 4:14–16, Hebrews 9:12–14, 22, 1 Peter 1:18–19, and 1 John 3:4–5.

Was Jesus able to pay the ransom price? What made His shed blood worthy to redeem us from our sins?

Yes! His sinless, unblemished shed blood on the cross was the ransom price paid that satisfied God's wrath against the sins of the whole world (Hebrews 2:17 and 1 John 2:2).

Boaz loved Ruth and redeemed her with money so that she could become his wife, but we were not redeemed with perishable things such as silver or gold. We have been eternally redeemed with the precious blood of Jesus!

DISCUSSION QUESTIONS:

John 3:16–17 are very popular verses. Now that we have a fresh understanding of Jesus' work on the cross, how do these verses touch you more personally? What do you learn about God's heart in them?

God loved us so much that He Himself provided the ransom price for our sins. God sent His Son into the world to purchase for Himself a bride, the church, with His own unblemished blood.

Jesus was willing and able to pay the redemption price, which was free to us, but came at a great cost to Him!

Oh, what a glorious gift!

"Thanks be to God for his inexpressible gift!" —2 Corinthians 9:15

Let's pause to pray and give thanks to our great Redeemer, Jesus Christ!

Verse of the Day:

May the God of hope fill you with

all joy and peace in believing,

so that by the power of the Holy Spirit

you may abound in hope.

Romans 15:13

Day 5: Amazing Love

Begin with prayer.

We have reached the final day of our study in the book of Ruth, and today's reading and conclusions are amazing! This is like the finale of a fireworks show—it's simply the best! But before we begin, I want to look back for a moment.

Ruth's story was one of loss, loyalty, love, family lineage...and hope!

If you love God and want His will for your life, then you are like Ruth.

If you have suffered the loss of a loved one or a dream, then you are like Ruth.

If you have ever felt like your past might hold you back, then you are like Ruth.

And if you believe redemption is possible for your life no matter what you've been through, then you are like Ruth.

Hold onto hope!

Remember that friendships change lives.

Remember that you don't have to have a perfect family to be used by God. Jesus' family line is filled with people who are not perfect.

Remember that we are foreigners in this world because our citizenship is in heaven.

Remember that nothing in your life happens by accident.

You are a part of the greatest love story of all time, and that love story is between you and your kinsman-redeemer, Jesus. He was willing to pay the price for you, and He loves you.

So let's look at the final qualification.

The sixth and final qualification of the kinsman-redeemer was his responsibility to avenge the murder of a close blood relative.

Let's review. What were God's instructions to Israel when innocent blood had been shed? Read Genesis 9:6. How was the blood of the murdered person to be compensated for?

Because God created man in His own image, when a human life was taken, the murderer was to be put to death.

In Numbers 35:19, who does Scripture say was to carry out this penalty for the intentional taking of a human life?

The close relative, the kinsman-redeemer, was to avenge and put to death the murderer. It was his duty to act as the blood avenger.

We have seen that Jesus left the glories of heaven to take on human flesh so that He could be our close relative, our kinsman-redeemer, and act as our blood avenger.

Read John 8:44, Romans 3:23, and Romans 5:12. When was mankind murdered, and who murdered him?

Satan is a liar and a murderer. He was a murderer from the beginning when he entered the Garden of Eden and brought about the fall of man. Death came through sin and has spread to all men because *"all have sinned and fall short of the glory of God."* Satan brought death to Adam and Eve and to every human being ever since.

Who is responsible to act as our blood avenger and kill the devil, the murderer of mankind?

Our kinsman-redeemer, Jesus Christ, is our blood avenger because He became a close relative when He became a man.

This event is yet future, but ultimately a time is coming when God is going to avenge the blood of His people, Israel. What do you learn in Joel 3:11–21, especially verses 19–21?

God will act as the blood avenger for Israel. These verses are referring to when Jesus Christ returns to earth a second time. The nations are going to be judged by God for the way they have treated God's people, Israel. God will avenge the innocent blood that has been shed in Judah and Jerusalem.

Look up Revelation 19:11–20:10. What do you learn about the final avenging of the blood of the bride of Christ, the church? What about Satan? When will he be destroyed?

Once again, we are speaking of the future. Our kinsman-redeemer, Jesus Christ, is going to return from heaven to earth in all His glory!

Jesus is coming in righteous judgment to destroy the wicked, to defeat Satan, and to establish His kingdom and take control of the earth. Satan will be bound for 1000 years, during which time the Lord and His saints will rule and reign upon the earth. There will be one final attempt at rebellion by Satan against God, but it will fail. Satan will then be cast into the lake of fire where he will be tormented day and night forever.

Those of us who have put our faith in the Lord Jesus Christ will be eternally blessed to enter His kingdom where we will live with our kinsman-redeemer, our Bridegroom, the King of Kings, and Lord of Lords, giving praise and worship to our great God and Savior, Jesus Christ, the Messiah, forever and ever!

"AMEN. COME, LORD JESUS!" —Revelation 22:20

Isn't this so exciting? What amazing love!

Jesus Christ truly is our kinsman-redeemer!

Just as Ruth put herself at the feet of Boaz and believed his promise to her, we too must humble ourselves, put ourselves at the foot of the cross, and believe the promises of God.

Naomi found hope again because the Lord had not left her without a redeemer.

Our only hope is found in Jesus.

DISCUSSION QUESTIONS:

What have you learned about God from reading the book of Ruth?

What have you learned about your own life from reading the book of Ruth?

Romans 15:13 says, *"May the God of hope fill you with all joy and peace in believing, so that by the power of the Holy Spirit you may abound in hope."*

Praise God, He has not left us without a Redeemer!

Our hope is in Him, and Him alone.

Our King and Redeemer is coming soon!

He loves you so.

Keep walking with the King.

Made in the USA
Monee, IL
05 October 2021